D0152906

& Language

blic Library

NCE

178 rev. 1-94

Izaak Walton

Twayne's English Authors Series

Arthur F. Kinney, Editor

University of Massachusetts, Amherst

TEAS 548

IZAAK WALTON
Courtesy of the National Portrait Gallery, London

Izaak Walton

P. G. Stanwood

University of British Columbia

Twayne Publishers
An Imprint of Simon & Schuster Macmillan
New York

Prentice Hall International
London • Mexico City • New Delhi • Singapore • Sydney • Toronto

Twayne's English Authors Series No. 548

Izaak Walton
Paul G. Stanwood

Twayne Publishers
An Imprint of Simon & Schuster Macmillan
1633 Broadway
New York, NY 10019

Library of Congress Cataloging-in-Publication Data
Stanwood, P. G.
    Izaak Walton / Paul G. Stanwood.
        p. cm. — (Twayne's English authors series ; no. 548)
    Includes bibliographical references (p.   ) and index.
    ISBN 0-8057-7052-6 (hardc)
    1. Walton, Izaak, 1593–1683—Literary art. 2. English prose
literature—Early modern, 1500–1700—History and criticism.
3. Fishing—England—Historiography. 4. Biography as a literary
form. I. Title.   II. Series: Twayne's English authors series ;
TEAS no. 548.
PR3757.W6Z88 1998
828'.309—dc21   97-41986
                                                                                  CIP

This paper meets the requirements of ANSI/NISO Z3948–1992 (Permanence of Paper).

10 9 8 7 6 5 4 3 2 1

Printed in the United States of America

For Dorothy

Contents

Editor's Note

Paul G. Stanwood's sensitive account of Izaak Walton tells how an unknown linen draper in London came to write "the best pastoral in the language," as William Hazlitt has noted, and to become "the outstanding biographer of his age." Walton is best known today as the author of *The Compleat Angler,* a poetic yet instructive account of fishing (angling) framed by a keen sense of the society and religious perspective (Anglicanism) that informs it. The book, published in more than 400 editions, has almost never been out of print since it was first published in 1653: it is the epitome of English Renaissance prose.

But Walton, Stanwood notes, should also be seen as England's first important biographer, writing what have been for centuries our basic accounts of the lives of John Donne, George Herbert, Richard Hooker, and others. Walton writes in his preface to his *Life of Donne,* "When I heard that sad news [of his death], and heard also that these Sermons were to be printed, and want the Authors Life, which I thought to be very remarkable: Indignation or grief (indeed I know not which) transported me so far, that I reviewed my forsaken-Collections, and resolv'd the World should see the best plain Picture of the Authors Life that my artless Pensil, guided by the hand of truth, could present to it." Walton's combination here, as elsewhere, of myth, legend, and fact has dominated critical perceptions of Donne and of others he chose to honor, and his biographies were soon attached to publications of their subjects' works. In his elegant and lucid commentary of Walton's life and writing, Stanwood matches the charm and the indelible style of his subject, who, through the centuries, so impressed Dr. Johnson, Wordsworth, Coleridge, and other great English writers who themselves drew on his prose for their own.

Arthur F. Kinney

Preface

This study attempts to introduce the life of one of the most remarkable yet unprepossessing figures of the late English Renaissance. Izaak Walton (1593–1683) had no special advantages of family or education, though his two marriages linked him first with the Cranmers and second with the Kens: the great Elizabethan archbishop and martyr, on the one side, and the notable High Church Restoration bishop, on the other. Yet Walton's own background was undistinguished and his formal learning limited to the local schools of Stafford, a small midland town of no special significance in the seventeenth century. As a very young man, he moved to London, where he was apprenticed as a linen draper, or sempster, and where through the force of an extremely inquisitive and genial personality he managed to ingratiate himself among the wittiest, most fashionable, and most learned persons of the great city. Among his friends and acquaintances were such writers as Michael Drayton, Ben Jonson, John Donne, and Sir Henry Wotton, and a host of eminent clergymen, including Henry King, George Morley, and Gilbert Sheldon.

Walton's circle held him in high esteem, and Walton's own literary talent flourished to the extent that he was able to write a new kind of biography, something that combined hagiography, true-to-life detail, colorful anecdote, informal dialogue, and historical interpretation. His love of order and serenity, his dislike of contention and revolution in both church and state, and his friendship with so many important (and eminently conservative) clergymen easily put him on the royalist side during the civil strife of the times. Thus his *Lives,* written, revised, and regularly published during the 40 years from 1640, reflect the attitudes of a highly partial insider, who nevertheless manages to seem objective and persuasive.

After surveying his life, I describe how Walton makes his biographies so convincing, so aesthetically pleasing, and indeed so memorializing. His own contemporaries especially valued his *Lives*—of John Donne, Sir Henry Wotton, Richard Hooker, George Herbert, and Robert Sanderson—often for reasons that are not obvious to later readers. I therefore wished to describe the particular circumstances that Walton was addressing in these *Lives* in order to contextualize them. No history is possible without a point of view, and I have tried to clarify in each of

Walton's life studies the nature and focus of his perception of the persons and events that touched him.

Although Walton was especially celebrated in his own time for his *Lives* of five very different but closely connected personalities, later generations have more generously appreciated his fishing manual, *The Compleat Angler*. Recent critics have tried to read this book as if it were principally a prose pastoral, a return to a kind of Vergilian georgic. Others have discovered predominantly political and ecclesiastical themes in the work, as if Walton were really writing allegorically about the wars and revolutions of seventeenth-century England. My view is that *The Compleat Angler* is fundamentally a book about fish and fishing that is decidedly set in a real English countryside; but it is more than this, for country pleasures are both real and imagined. The English ideal—at least since Walton's time, and probably long before—is to live in a thatched cottage near a pretty stream, an ideal that for some has always been possible to obtain. Walton writes of an England that never was but is always possible, the same England that Constable and Turner and the landscape painters later demonstrated in their own way. *The Compleat Angler* is, then, a book about angling that can be seen as a comment on its times, but it is a work that lives through all times where there is right perception, or (in the scriptural phrase) "open vision." We must not reduce the *Angler* to a single species, for Walton delights in providing a number of views, of the countryside, of rivers, of fish, of people, of literary reflections, even of songs and poetry. The richness of the book lies in its variety and its elusiveness, and also in its further relationship with the *Lives,* an important point that I believe is unique to my study.

I close with a long chapter on Walton's continuing fame and influence, for few writers in English have enjoyed such long and diverse popularity amidst the whirligigs of time and fortune. Walton's long life of nearly 90 years embraced the last years of Elizabeth I, the reigns of James I and his son Charles I, the years of Cromwell, and most of Charles II's time. Such an abundant life, lived mainly at the center of events in London itself, is richly instructive. Largely detached from political turmoils although profoundly affected by them, Walton provides an unusual chance for us to visit and to learn from the past, and to know more surely that the quality of change lies in changelessness.

Acknowledgments

I am grateful to the most helpful staff of the University of British Columbia Library, particularly to Lee Perry, curator of the Hawthorn Collection of Waltoniana; to the Interlibrary Loan and Reference Divisions, especially to Keith Bunnell; and also to Dr. Joseph Black, former curator of the Centre for Reformation and Renaissance Studies at Victoria College at the University of Toronto. I am chiefly thankful to Mary Ellen Henley, my doctoral research assistant, who has supported this study from its beginning and whose tenacious bibliographical inquiries and superb organizational skills enabled me to write most of the concluding chapter.

The frontispiece, which reproduces the painting by Jacob Huysmans (1633?–1696) of Izaak Walton, appears courtesy of the National Portrait Gallery, London. The autograph letter from Izaak Walton to Dorothy Smith of 21 March 1661 is reproduced by kind permission of the Houghton Library, Harvard University (shelf mark MS Eng 771).

I am as always most indebted to my wife, to whom I dedicate this book.

Chronology

1593–1598   September, Izaak Walton born in Stafford, to Gervase, a tippler, and Anne; baptized 21 September at St. Mary's, Stafford; Gervase dies in 1597, and Anne remarries in 1598; educated at the Edward VI Grammar School in Stafford.

?1608   Moves to London and lives with his sister, Anne, wife of Thomas Grinsell, a prosperous linen draper, to whom Walton is apprenticed in the parish of St. Dunstan's-in-the West.

?1612   Meets Samuel Page, Ben Jonson, Michael Drayton, and other literary figures.

1613   "S.P." [Samuel Page] dedicates *The Love of Amos and Laura* to "Iz. Wa." in a volume of verse printed by Richard Hawkins, a neighbor of his brother-in-law Grinsell.

1618   On Grinsell's recommendation, becomes a freeman of the Ironmongers' Company on 12 November.

1626   Marries Rachel Floud, daughter of William Floud and Susannah (Cranmer) Floud; continues to live in Chancery Lane; increasingly prosperous in trade and active in the parish of St. Dunstan's, to which John Donne had been preferred in March 1624; describes himself as Donne's "convert"; becomes acquainted with Henry Wotton and other members of Donne's circle of friends.

1627   Hears Donne preach at the funeral of George Herbert's mother, Magdalen, Lady Danvers, in Chelsea.

1631   Present at Donne's deathbed; friendship with George Morley, later bishop of Winchester.

1633   Publishes an elegy on the death of Donne in the first edition of Donne's poems.

1635 Revises his elegy on Donne; composes a poem on Donne's portrait; edits a selection of letters for the second edition of the poems.

1639 Death of Wotton.

1640 Completes the *Life of Donne* in February and publishes it in *LXXX Sermons Preached by that Learned and Reverend Divine, John Donne;* Parliament seizes control of Walton's company; his wife, Rachel, dies; his seventh and only remaining child by Rachel dies two years later.

1644 Leaves residency at St. Dunstan's and Chancery Lane, moves to Clerkenwell.

1647 Marries Anne Ken at St. James', Clerkenwell.

1651 "The Life of Sir Henry Wotton" published in *Reliquiae Wottonianae;* transports part of the Garter regalia lost by Charles II at Worcester to the Tower of London.

1653 *The Compleat Angler.*

1655 Retires with Anne and their three children to Staffordshire; second edition of *The Compleat Angler.*

1660 Returns to London; eclogue on the king's return.

1661 *The Compleat Angler,* third edition; moves to Worcester as steward to the newly consecrated bishop, George Morley; Anne Walton dies.

1662 Moves to Winchester with his children following Morley's translation to that see.

1664 *The Compleat Angler,* third edition, reissued.

1665 *The Life of Mr. Richard Hooker;* daughter Anne marries Dr. William Hawkins, a prebendary of Winchester Cathedral.

1668 *The Compleat Angler,* fourth edition.

1670 *The Life of Mr. George Herbert; The Lives of Dr. John Donne, Sir Henry Wotton, Mr. Richard Hooker, Mr. George Herbert.*

1675 *Lives* (with final additions to *Donne, Herbert,* and *Hooker*).

Chapter One
Walton's Life and Times

Born in 1593, the same year as George Herbert and one of the last years of Elizabeth's reign, yet of humble origins and possessing little formal education, Izaak Walton came to know many of the same persons as the aristocratic Herbert, including John Donne. Although Herbert died quite young, in 1633, Walton lived into his 90th year, an observer and survivor of wars and revolution. Walton's life, about which he was always reticent and revealed few details, appears relatively serene and undramatic, rarely marked by colorful incidents or adventures. From this distance, Walton seems the picture of composure and stability, but we cannot know how much his "study to be quiet" really cost him. The figure of "honest Izaak" that impressed his friends was perhaps the result of considerable emotional investment, and the supposed objectivity of his *Lives* in fact depends upon his own implicit self-portraiture. How Walton depicts and reflects his life and predispositions through his writing will become clear in subsequent chapters. But first I shall outline, so far as possible, the principal external events of his life.[1]

Izaak Walton's father, Gervase Walton of Yoxall, Staffordshire, was a tippler, that is, a person who kept an alehouse but did not serve meals or rent rooms. Gervase was married to Anne (b. ca. 1554, but of whom little else is known) sometime between 1570 and 1575. Their son Izaak was born in September 1593 and was baptized on 21 September 1593 in St. Mary's Church in Stafford, where Izaak's parents had moved by about 1591. Gervase Walton died on 11 February 1597, when Izaak was four years old. Anne subsequently married Humphrey Burne, an inn holder and baker, on 8 August 1598.

Gervase and Anne's children were Izaak, probably the youngest and last; a brother, Ambrose, buried 3 March 1596 (age unknown but greater than Izaak's); and a sister, Anne, who might have been his stepsister (that is, born of Humphrey Burne and Anne). Izaak's sister died in 1647. His mother died in 1623, and she was buried at St. Mary's, Stafford, on 23 May. Humphrey Burne, Izaak's stepfather, was buried on 16 March 1639.

1

Walton's education might have been in a "dame" school, which provided a kind of private tuition. But there was also a free grammar school in Stafford, established around 1545, which was originally known as St. Bertelin's and later as Edward VI Grammar School; it was housed in St. Bertelin's Church at the west end of the parish of St. Mary's. Izaak Walton might well have attended here, where there was a solitary schoolmaster, perhaps a chantry priest, who taught elementary and grammar school subjects. In any case, young Izaak had no more formal education than what he acquired in Stafford.[2]

Walton's sister, Anne, married Thomas Grinsell of London around 1608, and shortly after this time, Walton took up residence with the Grinsells on Chancery Lane. In about 1611, Walton was apprenticed to Grinsell, probably a draper, who was a member of the Ironmongers' Company; and Walton himself, having served his apprenticeship, was admitted to the company in November 1618.

A poem by Samuel Page, *The Love of Amos and Laura*, published in 1613, contains prefatory verses addressed to Walton; these lines reveal that Walton already had some reputation as a writer or a friend of writers. Page was succeeded as vicar of St. Nicholas's Church, Deptford, by Henry Valentine, who married Sara Grinsell, the daughter of Walton's sister. It is interesting to note that Page had contributed verses to the prefatory poems to Coryat's *Crudities* (1611). Contributors to those poems formed a remarkable group that also included Ben Jonson, John Donne, Christopher Brooke (who had shared a room with Donne at Oxford and witnessed Donne's marriage to Anne More), Inigo Jones, Thomas Campion, John Davies of Hereford, Michael Drayton, John Harrington, Henry Goodyer, and others. It is difficult to know to what extent Walton was acquainted with these poets and wits-about-town, but he seems certainly to have had very early exposure to them all.

Walton's brother-in-law Thomas Grinsell died in 1644 and his wife (Walton's sister), Anne, in 1647. Walton had long since left his residence with them when he married Rachel Floud on 27 December 1626 in the parish of St. Dunstan's-in-the-West, where Walton had established residence and owned property. Rachel Floud's father was William Floud of Canterbury, who had married Susannah Cranmer in 1598. Walton's mother-in-law came from a distinguished family, being a grandniece of Archbishop Cranmer and a sister of George Cranmer, who was a friend of Richard Hooker. Susannah's sister was Dorothy Cranmer, who first married Dr. John Spenser, president of Corpus Christi College,

Oxford, and later Richard Field, friend of Hooker, dean of Gloucester, and author of the important controversial work *Of the Church* (1606–1610, 1628, 1635). Walton's connections with his wife's family were to prove of lasting significance, though Rachel died 22 August 1640, having borne Walton seven children, none of whom survived him: (1) Izaak (b. 19 December 1627, d. 28 March 1631), (2) John (b. 23 July 1629, d. the same year?), (3) Thomas (b. 20 January 1631, d. 6 March 1631), (4) Henry (b. 12 October 1632, d. five days later), (5) Henry (b. 21 March 1634, d. 4 December 1634), (6) William (b. 1637?, d. August 1637), and (7) Anne (b. 10 July 1640, d. 11 May 1642).

Although Walton, like Thomas Grinsell, was a member of the Ironmongers' Company, he was a linen draper and sempster, that is, a man who sold cloth and also fashioned it into clothing, including, probably, hats. Being a member of the Ironmongers' indicated simply that he was a freeman of the livery company that bears this name and thus a "citizen" of London. Walton was a tradesman in cloth, never an ironmonger, though he was a member of the latter profession's guild and rose to some prominence in it. As a guildsman, he took part in two pageants in honor of the lord mayor of London, the first as a "batchelor in foins" (that is, in a fur-trimmed costume) in November 1629, the second in 1635. He was advanced to junior warden of the yeomanry in the fall of 1637 and in the following year to senior warden, offices that required him to advise members of meetings, collect fines, and perform various business. In 1641, Walton was assessed £3 as his portion of the huge levy of £40,000 placed upon the Ironmongers' and other city companies by the lord mayor for the conduct of parliamentary affairs. Walton's recorded connection with the Ironmongers' Company ends with this date, and his whereabouts are difficult to trace for the next several years. He seems to have left Chancery Lane around 1643, and if Anthony à Wood is to be believed, he left London then, "(at which time he found it dangerous for honest men to be there,) . . . and lived sometimes at Stafford, and elsewhere, but mostly in the Families of the eminent Clergymen of England, of whom he was much beloved" (Wood, 1:264–65).

While prospering in his business, Walton had also become more prominent in his parish and church of St. Dunstan's, serving in a variety of offices and finally being elected to the vestry in February 1640, meetings of which he attended faithfully for the next three years. We recall that John Donne presided as vicar at St. Dunstan's beginning in March 1624 (two and a half years after his appointment as dean of St. Paul's) and that Walton knew him as a parishioner; it is possible that Walton had some earlier contact with him and his circle of poets and writers, which would have included Henry King (1592–1669), whose father, John, had ordained Donne in 1615. Walton was involved in the publication of the first collected edition of Donne's *Poems* (1633), possibly as its editor—a supposition based on Walton's relationship with the publisher, John Marriot of Fleet Street. Marriot was Walton's neighbor, friend, and (with his son Richard) the publisher of Walton's own books. Walton contributed one of the elegies on Donne in this edition (along with Henry King, Sir Lucius Cary, Thomas Carew, and others), and in the second edition of 1635 he provided eight lines that appear beneath the engraving of the young Donne by William Marshall, which together form the frontispiece, entitled "On a Portrait of Donne Taken in his Eighteenth Year," of this new edition:

> This was for youth, Strength, Mirth, and wit that Time
> Most count their golden Age; but 'twas not thine.
> Thine was thy later yeares, so much refind
> From youths Drosse, Mirth & wit; as thy pure mind
> Thought (like the Angels) nothing but the Praise
> Of thy Creator, in those last, best Dayes.
> Witness this Booke, (thy Embleme) which begins
> With Love; but endes, with Sighes, & Teares for sinns.

Walton's emphasis on Donne's later life and on his death is significant and quite in harmony with his biography, which appeared as a preface to Donne's *LXXX Sermons* (1640) and especially to the much-expanded revision of the *Life* of 1658; in the latter volume, a telling motto from Ecclesiasticus 48:14 appears on the title page: "He did wonders in his life, and at his death his works were marvelous."

Walton's literary career and friendships were by now well established, and his innate conservatism and royalist sympathies were sustained through his association with many notable churchmen, acquired partly through his Cranmer family connections. Walton apparently took no very active part in the Civil Wars, and in leaving Chancery Lane, he managed to remain in some obscurity, living in nearby Clerkenwell and probably also for some time in his former residence of Stafford. Walton records in his *Life of Sanderson* (1678), written during the Restoration in the last years of his life, that "about this time the Bishop of *Canterbury* having been by an unknown Law condemned to die, and the execution suspended for some days, many of the malicious Citizens fearing his pardon, shut up their Shops, professing not to open them till Justice was executed. This malice and madness is scarce credible, but I saw it."[3] Walton is of course recalling the execution of William Laud on 10 January 1645, which he may indeed have witnessed, though his testimony here is ambiguous, representing merely general if acute awareness.

We know that Walton was in Clerkenwell in 1647, for on 23 April of that year he was married for the second time, as the Register of Marriages of the Parish of St. James records. His second wife was Anne Ken, the eldest daughter of Thomas Ken, attorney-at-law, of Furnivall's Inn, London, and of Ken's first wife, Jane, daughter of Rowland Hughes of Essenden. This Anne, who was born around 1612 (she was about 35 and Walton 54 when they were married), had acquired some nine half brothers and half sisters when, after the death of her mother, her father remarried. One of these half brothers was the younger Thomas Ken (1637–1711), who was to become the Restoration bishop of Bath and Wells (1684), thus providing Walton with a further link to an ecclesiastical family. About Anne Ken we know almost nothing, except that she and Walton had three children: Ann (b. 11 March 1648), Isaac (b. 10 February 1650 and died four months later), and a second son, also Isaac (b. 7 September 1651). Walton's eighth son was to survive him and become a canon of Salisbury; he died, never having married, in 1719. Ann married Dr. William Hawkins, a prebendary of Winchester during the Restoration and also rector of Droxford, Hampshire.

Walton's movements during the late 1640s and the Interregnum are rather uncertain, but in 1651 he managed the most celebrated of his exploits, a minor but remarkable intervention in the political events of his time. Walton safely transported a part of the Garter regalia, left behind at the battle of Worcester, to the Tower of London. This deed is known through Elias Ashmole, a friend of Walton's, who related it in his *History of the Order of the Garter:*

> Nor will it be unfitly here remembered, by what good fortune the present sovereign's lesser *George*, set with fair diamonds, was preserved, after the defeat given to the Scotch forces at *Worcester, ann.* 4 Car. II [3 September 1651]. Among the rest of his attendants then dispersed, Colonel *Blague* was one; who taking shelter at *Blore-pipe-house* in *Staffordshire,* where one Mr. *George Barlow* then dwelt, delivered his wife this *George* to secure. Within a week after Mr. *Barlow* himself carried it to *Robert Mil-*

ward, Esq.; he being then a prisoner to the parliament, in the garrison of *Stafford;* and by this means was it happily preserved and restored: for not long after he delivered it to Mr. *Isaac Walton* (a man well known, and as well beloved of all good men; and will be better known to posterity by his ingenious pen . . .) to be given to Colonel *Blague,* then a prisoner in the *Tower;* who, considering it had already past so many dangers, was persuaded it could yet secure one hazardous attempt of his own; and thereupon leaving the *Tower,* without leavetaking, hasted the presentation of it to the present sovereign's hand.[4]

Walton was evidently regarded as a trustworthy and reliable courier. Ashmole's account also suggests that Walton was in or near Stafford at this time, or at least able to move freely between there and London; but one must reckon the distances and the difficulty of travel: from London to Worcester is more than 100 miles, and Stafford is another 40 miles north from there. Walton's move from St. Dunstan's-in-the-West, Fleet Street, to St. James's, Clerkenwell, had meant a change of parish and neighborhood, but the two places are separated by less than a mile. That Walton kept a kind of "headquarters" or some sort of establishment in Stafford while also frequently visiting London, as Arthur M. Coon has conjectured, seems to me unlikely and unnecessary. Walton remained principally in London throughout these years.

But his specific whereabouts are vague until the Restoration, even though we should assume that he remained chiefly in Clerkenwell, which would have been convenient and obvious; for Walton had a new family, and at the same time he continued to write. With the success of his *Life of Donne,* Walton turned to a second biography about his and Donne's old friend Sir Henry Wotton, at one time the ambassador to Venice and finally provost of Eton College. It is the end of the life that most interests Walton, as is typical of all the *Lives.* Richard Marriot, a friend of Walton's, was the publisher of *Reliquiae Wottonianae,* which included the *Life,* the work appearing first in 1651. Only two years later, in 1653, came the first edition of *The Compleat Angler.* Thus Walton had completed three works that share many features; yet the two biographies and the piscatory manual, in which both Wotton and Donne make appearances, were works in progress, for Walton continued to revise these works even as he began to write new ones. *The Compleat Angler* underwent extensive remodeling (not merely revising) over the next 23 years, with subsequent editions published in 1655, 1661, 1668, and 1676; there are four revisions of the *Life of Wotton* (1654, 1670,

1672, and 1675), and the *Life of Donne* fared similarly, with revised editions in 1658, 1670, and 1675.

The relationship of the poet Charles Cotton (1630–1687) and Izaak Walton was in the last years of Walton's life especially warm, Cotton regarding himself as a "son" to his "father" Izaak. The second part of *The Compleat Angler* of 1676, now called *The Universal Angler*, is testimony to this friendship, for Walton had invited Cotton to write "particular Directions for the taking of a Trout" for this fifth edition. The two exchanged complimentary letters at the time of publication, Cotton writing from Beresford, his seat in Derbyshire, in March, and Walton from London in April.[5] In this second part of *The Compleat Angler*, Cotton takes the role of "Piscator," the guide who gleaned knowledge from Walton himself, a man who "understands as much of fish and fishing as any man living": "I have the happiness to know his person, and to be intimately acquainted with him; and in him to know the worthiest man, and to enjoy the best and the truest friend any man ever had: . . . he gives me leave to call him Father, and I hope is not yet ashamed to own me for his adopted Son."[6] Cotton obviously felt a deep attachment to Walton, yet the affectionate terms with which he praises him are characteristic of other persons who write of Walton, for he invariably excited admiration and praise for his kindness and honesty.

At the Restoration, Walton composed a commendatory poem on the king's return—one of many such effusions popular at the time—which was printed in his friend Alexander Brome's *Songs and Other Poems* (1661). The sentiments, expressed as a dialogue in somewhat halting verse, are typical of a faithful royalist. Daman and Dorus are really one voice speaking in two parts, and they report Walton's own views:

> *Daman.*
> Hail happy day! Dorus sit down:
> Now let no sign, nor let a frown
> Lodge near thy heart, or on thy brow.
> The King! the King's return'd: and now
> Let's banish all sad thoughts and sing
> We have our Laws, and have our King.[7]

This pastoral continues predictably for another 41 lines, including the following:

> Let Rebel spirits sing; let those
> That like the Goths and Vandals rose
> To ruine families, and bring
> Contempt upon our Church, our King,
> And all that's dear to us, be sad.
>
> (11–15)

Others may have their turn of sadness, for Walton and his friends have endured theirs, and they can now rejoice in their freedom and once more rule: "We have our Laws, / God bless the King" (47).

During his early years in London, Walton had become widely acquainted with many of the leading figures of the day—writers, publishers, churchmen—through family and business relationships, and through an ever-widening pattern of associations connected with his parish of St. Dunstan's. Walton came to know Donne at that time, and through Donne, Sir Henry Wotton, and through Wotton, John Hales and members of the Great Tew circle, philosophically and theologically minded men who met at the estate near Oxford of Lucius Cary, second viscount Falkland (?1610–1643). This loosely gathered group, dedicated to the discussion of principles of toleration and irenicism, included Cary himself; Edward Hyde (1609–1674), later first earl of Clarendon; William Chillingworth (1602–1644), celebrated for his *Religion of Protestants a Safe Way to Salvation* (1638); George Morley (1597–1684); and others. Although Walton may not have visited Great Tew—there is no record of his having done so—he was certainly on familiar terms with those who did visit there.[8]

Morley was of special importance, for he became one of Walton's closest friends, and like many members of Great Tew, he rose to great prominence during the Restoration. Having been ejected from Mildenhall, Wiltshire, in 1641 for being a royalist, he went to Paris with the exiled court, where he conducted services for Anglican exiles. Soon after his return to England in 1660, he became dean of Christ Church, Oxford, and later in the same year bishop of Worcester. He preached the coronation sermon for Charles II on 23 April 1661 and in the next year was translated to the much richer diocese of Winchester. Morley remembered his old friend and appointed him his personal steward in Worcester. Walton's second wife died in April 1662 in this place, where she is buried. Walton continued in Morley's employment and moved with him to Winchester, where he lived, perhaps staying for periods also at the episcopal residence at Farnham Castle or else at the diocesan house in Chelsea, London.

Walton's reputation as a biographer with sound views who was well known to all of the leading clergy of the Restoration resulted in his turning, rather by accident, to the writing of *The Life of Richard Hooker*. John Gauden, bishop of Exeter, had written a long and rambling life of Hooker to preface the first collected edition of Hooker's *Works* (1662). But the inadequacies of Gauden's biography inspired Gilbert Sheldon (1598–1677), archbishop of Canterbury from 1663, to ask Walton for a proper life of Hooker to accompany the next edition of the *Works* in 1665 and so to replace Gauden's defective version. During these years, Walton also wrote two more biographies—of George Herbert (1670, 1675) and of Robert Sanderson (1678, 1681). Walton might have planned to write lives of John Hales, for which he left some notes, and Henry Hammond, though his last principal work is the *Life of Sanderson*.[9] Meanwhile, Walton published anonymously *Love and Truth: in Two modest and peaceable Letters. Concerning The distempers of the present Times* (1680, though written in 1667 and 1679).

Walton had a lease, granted by Sheldon in 1662, for premises in Paternoster Row, which had burned in the Great Fire of 1666. On 1 July 1670, Walton presented a petition to the Court of Judicature for "Determination of Differences Touching Houses Burnt in London" (Coon, 273–74).[10] The petition asks for permission to rebuild the premises "so as he may be encouraged thereto by an increase of years to his term in being, and abatement of rent as the Court shall see is meet." The court granted Walton permission to rebuild, with a 60-year lease at the old rate of rent, and he evidently did rebuild, for his will refers to a "house and shop" in Paternoster Row.

Walton seems to have spent his final years in Droxford, with his daughter and son-in-law, who was the rector there. He must have visited also with his son, who in 1678 was appointed domestic chaplain to Seth Ward, bishop of Salisbury. On 16 October 1679 Bishop Morley granted Izaak Walton a 21-year lease of Northampton Farm, near Winchester, at an annual rental of £9.6.8. Walton still held the lease at his death and bequeathed it to his son. At about this time, on 22 November 1680, he wrote to John Aubrey his recollections of Ben Jonson at the request of the famous biographer and gossip, which Aubrey included in his brief life of the poet.[11] Walton was never idle, for along with the revising and reprinting of the *Lives*, there appeared in 1683, the year of his death, "A Pastoral History in smooth and easie Verse," called *Thealma and Clearchus*, attributed to John Chalkhill and prefaced by Walton.[12] Walton's will is dated 9 August 1683, when the work was begun, but

the will was signed and sealed on 24 October.[13] He refers to himself as
"of Winchester," where he was doubtless living at the time of his death
on 15 December 1683, during a severe frost. He was buried in Prior
Silkstede's Chapel, in the south aisle of Winchester Cathedral, where a
black marble slab above his body bears this inscription, reputedly written by his brother-in-law Thomas Ken:[14]

> HERE RESTETH THE BODY OF
>
> MR. IZAAC WALTON,
>
> WHO DIED THE 15TH OF DECEMBER
>
> 1683.
>
> Alas! he's gone before,
>
> Gone to return no more!
>
> Our panting breasts aspire,
>
> After their aged sire;
>
> Whose well-spent life did last
>
> Full ninety years and past.
>
> But now he hath begun
>
> That which will ne'er be done.
>
> Crown'd with eternal blisse,
>
> We wish our souls with his
>
> VOTIS MODESTIS SIC FLERUNT LIBERI.

**LETTER FROM IZAAK WALTON TO DOROTHY SMITH, 21 MARCH 1661.
THIS IS ONE OF THE VERY FEW SURVIVING LETTERS (OF ABOUT SIX)
IN IZAAK WALTON'S NEATLY FORMED SECRETARY HAND. THE RECIPI-
ENT OF THE LETTER IS UNKNOWN APART FROM WHAT THE LETTER
ITSELF DISCLOSES.[15]**

By permission of the Houghton Library, Harvard University, MS Eng 771.

Chapter Two

Walton the Biographer: Donne and Wotton

The Life of Dr. John Donne, Late Dean of St. Paul's Church, London

Biography and history depend upon a careful assessment of supposed facts, probable truths, and events, all filtered through a personal lens. Often called the first "literary" biographer in English, Izaak Walton is above all an interpreter of what he knows and likes, a disseminator not so much of recorded affairs but of culture and belief. We shall consider the general difficulties of the biographer's occupation, as Walton discovered and valued it, and examine also the complex cultural relationships that influenced Walton, particularly the associations that led to his interest in Donne and Wotton, and further directed his choice of subjects. This and the subsequent chapter will explore in detail the structure and plan of the different *Lives* and discuss their stylistic ingenuity and aesthetic appeal. Having considered Walton's five life studies, we shall then be well prepared to examine his avocation and life's work, *The Compleat Angler*—the fishing manual that serves as autobiography and cultural commentary.

One might say that Walton's literary career began almost as soon as he arrived in London around 1608. In the years shortly after he had settled in Chancery Lane with his sister and brother-in-law, he became acquainted with many of the most notable writers of the day, especially Ben Jonson and the members of the Mermaid circle. Evidently Walton was well liked and admired by all who knew him, surely not for his mean education but for his ingenuity and good sense; and he possessed an uncanny ability to ingratiate himself among persons who might notice him. He was not to disappoint anyone who might have seen in him literary promise. Although his publications were meager until he came to write the *Life of Donne* (1572–1631), this work was sufficient to establish his reputation as the outstanding biographer of his age. Walton was able to provide a view of Donne that accorded precisely with the attitudes of those who wished to celebrate him; Walton's achievement is the more striking for its seeming candor, its objectivity, its straightforward yet elegant style, and its utter lack of self-promotion. Walton makes a special virtue of his lack of learning, his humble origins, and his simplicity. Writers conventionally profess humility and impoverishment, but Walton's claims to simplicity, which he regularly makes, are entirely believable and support his credibility.

Walton came to compose the first of his *Lives* by accident, through the indolence of Sir Henry Wotton, who was, as Donne's old friend from their days together as students in Hart Hall, Oxford, best qualified to write of Donne and had indeed proposed to do so, not long after Donne's death in 1631. But Wotton was, in his own words, a man that "loves to do so little,"[1] and so he neglected the biography of Donne. Walton, who was Donne's parishioner at St. Dunstan's-in-the-West (and knew Wotton through Donne), wrote concernedly to Wotton as he watched his friend Richard Marriot prepare Donne's *LXXX Sermons* for publication, asking Wotton to carry forward his biography of Donne. Sometime early in 1639, perhaps in April, Wotton wrote to his "worthy friend" Izaak Walton:

> I am not able to yield any reason, no, not so much as may satisfy myself, why a most ingenuous Letter of yours hath lyen so long by me (as it were in lavender) without an answer, save this only, the pleasure I have taken in your style and conceptions, together with a meditation of the subject you propound, may seem to have cast me into a gentle slumber. But being now awaked, I do herein return you most hearty thanks for the kind prosecution of your first motion, touching a just office, due to the memory of our ever-memorable friend [John Donne]. To whose good fame, though it be needless to add anything (and my age considered, almost hopeless from my pen), yet I will endeavour to perform my promise, if it were but even for this cause, that in saying somewhat of the Life of so deserving a man I may perchance overlive mine own.[2]

Wotton died in December, leaving at most a few notes: "Death prevented his intentions," Walton wrote in his preface to the *Life of Donne*. He continues: "*When I heard that sad news, and heard also that these* Sermons *were to be printed, and want the* Authors Life, *which I thought to be very remarkable: Indignation or grief (indeed I know not which) transported me so far, that I reviewed my forsaken-Collections, and resolv'd the World should see the best plain Picture of the* Authors Life *that my artless Pensil, guided by the hand of truth, could present to it* (*Lives*, 21). Since Marriot was now anxious to bring out Donne's *LXXX Sermons* as soon as possible, Walton promptly set about writing his first biography—likely with little if any help from Wotton's supposed sketches—and finished it on 15 February 1640, just in time for inclusion as a preface to the *Sermons*.

In the general preface "To the Reader" of the 1675 collected edition of his *Lives*, Walton explains, in his characteristically self-deprecatory manner, the accidental nature of his biographical enterprise:

> *By my undertaking to collect some notes for Sir* Henry Wottons *writing the Life of* Dr. Donne, *and by Sir* Henry's *dying before he perform'd it, I became like those men that enter easily into a* Law-sute, *or a* quarrel, *and having begun, cannot make a fair retreat and be quiet, when they desire it. — And really, after such a manner, I became ingag'd, into a necessity of writing the* Life *of* Dr. Donne: *Contrary, to my first Intentions: And that begot a like necessity of writing the* Life *of his and my ever-honoured friend, Sir* Henry Wotton. (*Lives*, 5)

The *Life of Wotton* would follow *Donne* 11 years later; but Walton continued to write—*The Compleat Angler* followed shortly after *Wotton*—and he composed three more *Lives* during the Restoration, never ceasing to revise and tinker with everything he had already written. Walton's claim to naivete and simplicity is somewhat disingenuous, his seeming artlessness the result of painstaking and deliberate study. Perhaps Walton did begin his first biography in the way he has described, but he executed this task with extraordinary skill and genius, and discovered at the same time the pattern that he would continue to follow in the subsequent biographies.

Walton must have looked to his predecessors, writers of saints' lives, of eminent ecclesiastical persons, of political figures, and yet he creates something quite different.[3] He would of course have had available various compilations of medieval saints' lives, and especially Foxe's more recent and immensely popular *Book of Martyrs* (1563); but the rather repetitious nature of these lives, with their monotonous recitation of holy deeds, was not as appealing to Walton as the fuller kind of biography, sanctioned by Plutarch, its two-part structure including a detailed life and times, a character sketch, and a "parallel" life for the sake of contrast and for the convenient linking of separate studies. There was also the kind of biography, epitomized by George Cavendish (1500–1561?) and William Roper (1496–1578) in their respective lives of Cardinal Wolsey and Thomas More, that possesses a rising and falling action accented by a dramatic turn exactly at midpoint in the narrative. There is an ordering by which episodes in the first half are balanced by similar kinds of episodes in the second, or concluding, section.[4] Walton's gift is to adapt these various models in a unique and flexible manner that perfectly responds to his special needs and interests.

These interests might have been formed at first by accident, but Walton continued to foster them. It is no accident that all five of his *Lives* are about illustrious churchmen—even the worldly Wotton, Venetian ambassador and provost of Eton College, was in orders (necessitated by his appointment at Eton), a point that weighs significantly in Walton's account of him. Walton is obviously a sympathetic observer and recorder of them all, his study of Donne providing the usual pattern for the rest: description of early life, with selected illustrative events; a turning point, or climax, in the career; activity in a nobler calling; the accumulation of wisdom and contemplative benevolence; at last, decline into a holy death.

Walton begins his *Life of Donne* with an explanation and an apology, with which we are already in part familiar. He tells of the plan that Wotton should have written of Donne, "*a work worthy his undertaking . . . but then, Death prevented his intentions*" (*Lives*, 20–21). Walton sees himself as a most inappropriate substitute for Wotton, as one abjectly unworthy to lift his pen on Donne's behalf: "*Wonder indeed the Reader may, that I who profess my self artless should presume with my faint light to shew forth his Life whose very name makes it illustrious! but be this to the disadvantage of the person represented: Certain I am, it is to the advantage of the beholder, who shall here see the Authors Picture in a natural dress, which ought to beget faith in what is spoken: for he that wants skill to deceive, may safely be trusted*" (*Lives*, 21). In his self-conscious amazement, Walton promises to be truthful. How else can such a simple-hearted person act? One needs talent for deception. Donne himself might, if he could, approve these honest efforts:

> *If the Authors glorious spirit, which now is in Heaven; can have the leasure to look down and see me, the poorest, the meanest of all his friends, in the midst of this officious duty, confident I am, that he will not disdain this well-meant sacrifice to his memory: for, whilst his Conversation made me and many others happy below, I know his Humility and Gentleness was then eminent: and, I have heard Divines say, those Vertues that were but sparks upon Earth, become great and glorious flames in Heaven.* (*Lives*, 21–22)

Walton thus invests his *Life* with innocence and alleged accuracy.

Since this *Life* is Walton's first significant literary work, he may have been more than conventionally apologetic for its possible deficiencies or limitations. But between the first edition of 1640 and its third and last revision of 1675, Walton grew more confident in the selection and management of his material. Not only is the last version of the *Life of Donne* substantially longer than the first, it is also more decidedly reverent. David Novarr has carefully compared these several versions, noting that with the passage of time, Walton increasingly moved Donne closer to sainthood. Walton does not change the basic structure of the *Life*, nor does he add factual material that might reveal more of Donne's activities, nor does he recount Donne's accomplishments as a theologian or preacher. His additions are principally character-revealing anecdotes and incidents, with a missing date here, a forgotten name there; but overall the effect is one of heightening the original portrait.[5] Some vivid examples of these embellishments include Donne's vision, while in France, of his wife carrying her dead child; or the painting of himself in his shroud, which, in his last days, he ordered to be made and placed near his bedside. Such incidents, and more, have the effect of emphasizing Donne's spiritual sensitivity and transcendent piety.

Walton was, of course, initially writing the *Life of Donne*, as he was to write most of his *Lives*, as a preface to the author's works—the idea of collecting the *Lives* into an independent volume came much later. One might naturally expect an introduction to Donne's *LXXX Sermons* to concentrate on his clerical career, and surely not to highlight his earlier adventurous life, nor his secular poetry. Yet one would hardly know that Donne was celebrated for his poetry, whether secular or devotional, or that he was one of the most widely read poets of his generation, as the hundreds of manuscript collections that contain his poems seem certainly to prove. Walton's aim is to dignify Donne's early years so that he may be seen as worthy of the grave responsibilities that fell to him as the holy dean and preacher of St. Paul's.

To accomplish the task of writing such a biography, Walton carefully selects incidents from Donne's early years, leading smoothly toward the climax, or turning point, of his life, that is, his taking orders and gaining ecclesiastical preferment. The life naturally leads to death, but the progress is entirely upward; for Donne's death is shown to be his greatest triumph, the great action for which he had taken a lifetime to prepare. Little mention is made of Donne's travels with Essex, or of the efforts at court advancement. His employment as secretary to the lord keeper, Sir Thomas Egerton, is noted for its exemplary quality and usefulness, "his

Lordship . . . appointing him a place at his own Table, to which he
esteemed his Company and Discourse to be a great Ornament" (*Lives*,
26). Walton describes the end of this employment and of Donne's immediate hope for advancement in an extraordinarily deft account of his
elopement with Anne, niece of his patron and daughter of the eminent
but irascible Sir George More: "Love is a flattering mischief, that hath
denied aged and wise men a foresight of those evils that too often prove
to be the children of that blind father, a passion! that carries us to com-
mit *Errors* with as much ease as whirlwinds remove feathers, and begets
in us an unwearied industry to the attainment of what we desire. And
such an Industry did, notwithstanding much watchfulness against it,
bring them secretly together (I forbear to tell the manner how) and at
last to a marriage too, without the allowance of those friends, whose
approbation always was, and ever will be necessary, to make even a vertuous love become lawful" (*Lives*, 27–28). Sir George is depicted as a type
of "angry man," or father, who manages to separate Donne from his
employer: "Yet the Lord *Chancellor* said, *He parted with a Friend; and such a
Secretary as was fitter to serve a King then a Subject* (*Lives*, 29).

Donne entered now into a kind of retirement, "whose necessary and
daily expences were hardly reconcileable with his uncertain and narrow
estate" (*Lives*, 31). Walton here introduces an exchange of correspondence between Thomas Morton, later bishop of Durham (1632), and
Donne; letters regularly provide Walton with a means for advancing his
narrative. The chronology is confusing, for Walton recalls Morton's letter when he was appointed dean of Gloucester (1606), an office possessed of a benefice, which Morton is eager that Donne should occupy, if
only he might take orders. Walton does not mention that Donne had
probably assisted Morton in one or more of his anti-Romanist writings,
notably *Apologia Catholica* (1605), nor does Walton say anything about
Donne's own controversial work, *Ignatius His Conclave* (1611), a witty
satire on the Jesuits. Instead, he simply mentions in passing Donne's
Pseudo-Martyr (1610), a learned treatise designed to persuade Catholics
that they might take the Oath of Allegiance.

Walton has difficulty with the chronology of Donne's life, for he
introduces the Morton letter in order to demonstrate Donne's devotion
to the English church and his growing reputation within it. Walton earlier says that Donne at age 18 "had betrothed himself to no Religion
that might give him any other denomination than *a Christian*" (*Lives*,
25), yet around this remark are woven references to *Pseudo-Martyr*, in
which Donne is said to have begun surveying controverted points of

doctrine. When he received Morton's letter, however, we learn that "Mr. *Donne's* faint breath and perplext countenance gave a visible testimony of an inward conflict" (*Lives*, 33). This thread of the narrative is then abandoned, only to be resumed some pages later, after Walton recalls Donne's travel to France, in 1612, and the remarkable vision of his wife with a dead child in her arms. We return to 1610:

> About this time, there grew many disputes that concerned the *Oath of Supremacy* and *Allegiance*, in which the King had appeared, and engaged himself by his publick writings now extant: and, his Majesty discoursing with Mr. *Donne*, concerning many of the reasons which are usually urged against the taking of those Oaths; apprehended, such a validity and clearness in his stating the Questions, and his Answers to them, that his Majesty commanded him to bestow some time in drawing the Arguments into a method, and then to write his Answers to them: and, having done that, not to send, but be his own messenger and bring them to him. To this he presently and diligently applied himself, and, within six weeks brought them to him under his own handwriting, as they be now printed; the Book bearing the name of *Pseudo-martyr*, printed *anno* 1610. (*Lives*, 44–45)

On account of this book, the king determined that Donne should enter the ministry, Walton says; but Donne continued to be doubtful, wrestling with his supposed insufficiency and unfitness: "But God who is able to prevail, wrestled with him, as the *Angel* did with *Jacob, and marked him;* mark'd him for his own; mark'd him with a blessing; a blessing of obedience to the motions of his blessed Spirit. And then, as he had formerly asked God with *Moses, Who am I?* So now being inspired with an apprehension of Gods particular mercy to him, in the Kings and other solicitations of him, he came to ask *King Davids* thankful question, *Lord, who am I, that thou art so mindful of me?*" (*Lives*, 46–47). Walton's climactic relation of Donne's "conversion" is one of the most memorable passages in all the *Lives*, for it not only marks the moment of the anticipated turning point of his interpretation of Donne's life but also readies us for all that must inevitably follow.

Donne's youth and early career form one side of Walton's *Life;* the modern saint, posed in his shroud, is at the other side—the beginning and the ending. Although Donne did not take orders until 1615 (at the age of 43, 16 years before he died), Walton wants us to recognize a particular kind of figure, a person whose prototype is St. Augustine, who turned from a worldly to a religious life, a point that Walton makes explicit: "Now the *English Church* had gain'd a second St. *Austine*, for, I think, none was so like him before his Conversion: none so like St. *Ambrose* after it: and if his youth had the infirmities of the one, his age had the excellencies of the other; the learning and holiness of both" (*Lives*, 48). Now his learning and his thoughts are "concentred in Divinity," and his first sermon leads Walton to describe his typical homiletic style and pulpit personality in cogent and impressive terms, for Donne was "a Preacher in earnest weeping sometimes for his Auditory, sometimes with them: always preaching to himself, like an Angel from a cloud, but in none; carrying some, as St. *Paul* was, to Heaven in holy raptures, and inticing others by a sacred Art and Courtship to amend their lives; here picturing a vice so as to make it ugly to those that practised it; and a vertue so, as to make it be beloved even by those that lov'd it not; and all this with a most particular grace and an unexpressible addition of comeliness" (*Lives*, 49). In the succeeding years, Walton tells us, Donne lived in retirement—especially after the death of his wife (in 1617), in whose grave he buried "all his earthly joys" (*Lives*, 51); and yet Walton tells us much later that "his marriage was the remarkable error of his life" (*Lives*, 60), which he repented. But his life was "a continued study," the composition of his sermons his major preoccupation. Walton's vividly sympathetic description of this activity is well known and probably accurate:

> as he usually preached once a week, if not oftner, so after his Sermon he never gave his eyes rest, till he had chosen out a new Text, and that night cast his Sermon into a form, and his Text into divisions; and the next day betook himself to consult the Fathers, and so commit his meditations to his memory, which was excellent. But upon Saturday he usually gave himself and his mind a rest from the weary burthen of his weeks meditations, and usually spent that day in visitation of friends, or some other diversions of his thoughts; and would say, that *he gave both his body and mind that refreshment, that he might be enabled to do the work of the day following, not faintly, but with courage and chearfulness.* (*Lives*, 67)

A lasting picture of Donne is everywhere carefully and subtly delineated, the figure of the pious churchman sharply contrasted with the earlier courtier, whose experiences now are but a memory submerged in a stricter and better life.

Walton tells us of Donne's failing health, reports his will, then gives the notable and compelling story of his posing in his shroud:

Several Charcole-fires being first made in his Study, he brought with him into that place his winding-sheet in his hand, and, having put off all his cloaths, had this sheet put on him, and tyed with knots at his head and feet, and his hands so placed, as dead bodies are usually fitted to be shrowded and put into their Coffin, or grave. Upon this *Vrn* he thus stood with his eyes shut, and with so much of the sheet turned aside as might shew his lean, pale, and death-like face, which was purposely turned toward the East, from whence he expected the second coming of his and our Saviour Jesus. (*Lives*, 78)

Walton says that Donne ordered the resulting portrait to be set by his bedside, where he was able to meditate on it hourly until his death.[6] This picture remains with us, too, as a remembrance of Donne; but Walton reminds us of the picture drawn of Donne when he was a youth, thus setting the two contrasting icons before us. Yet some days were to pass before the death of "this memorable man" (*Lives*, 82), whose dying was itself an inspiration.

In the Chapter Library of Salisbury Cathedral is Walton's copy of *Eusebius, Socrates, and Evagrius, Ecclesiastical Histories* (London, 1636), in which he made a number of notes, probably for his biography of Donne.[7] He writes, "At his conversion take out of Jeremy the ways of man are not in his owne powr"; the idea, recalling perhaps Jeremiah 7:23 or Lamentations 3:40, certainly lies behind Walton's account of Donne's decision at last to take orders. Moreover, Walton notes, "vew doc cozens devotions" and "doc taylers living and dying." The first is a reference to John Cosin, author of *A Collection of Private Devotions, or The Hours of Prayer* (1627), a celebrated compilation that reflects the Laudian and High Church ethos. It includes offices and prayers "at the hour of death" and "at the point of death." Walton seems not to have borrowed directly from Cosin, but he would have found corroboration in him for the prayerful account of the last scenes of Donne's life. But Jeremy Taylor's *Holy Living* (1650) and *Holy Dying* (1651) together provide a very close analogue to Walton's lingering depiction of Donne's death. Walton, of course, could not have seen Taylor's books until he came to revise his *Life of Donne* in 1658; but it is this edition that contains the scene of Donne in his shroud and that gives special emphasis to Donne's art of dying well, the grand theme of *Holy Dying*. One might well read Taylor alongside Walton: "We who are alive should so live, and by the actions of Religion attend the coming of the day of the Lord, that we neither be surprized, nor leave our duties imperfect, nor our sins uncanceled, nor our persons unreconciled, nor God unappeased; but that when we descend to our graves we may rest in the bosome of the Lord, till the mansions be prepared, where we shall sing and feast eternally."[8] Taylor's plangent, carefully orchestrated style is similar to Walton's typical mode. With vivid expressiveness, Walton desires to exalt Donne's life in his death and to bring his end back to its starting point, as if to draw a circle.

The Life of Sir Henry Wotton, Late Provost of Eaton College

The image of the circle appealed to Walton, and when he concludes the life of his old friend Sir Henry Wotton (1568–1639), he writes pointedly:

> And thus the Circle of Sir *Henry Wotton*'s Life—(that Circle which began at *Bocton*, and in the *Circumference* thereof, did first touch at *Winchester-School*, then at *Oxford*, and after upon so many remarkable parts and passages in *Christendom*) That *Circle* of his *Life*, was by *Death* thus closed up and compleated, in the seventy and second year of his *Age*, at *Eaton Colledge*, where, according to his *Will*, he now lies buried, with his Motto on a plain Gravestone over him; dying worthy of his Name and *Family*, worthy of the love and favour of so many *Princes*, and Persons of eminent *Wisdom* and *Learning*, worthy of the trust committed unto him, for the Service of his *Prince* and *Countrey*. (*Lives*, 151)

Walton thus summarizes Wotton's long career while demonstrating its orderly pattern and compass. Although most of Wotton's years were engaged in secular employments, Walton still leads him from an adventurous diplomatic life to a wise and contemplative old age: the one has prepared him for the other.

Walton seems to have intended his *Life of Wotton* as a memorial to a warm friendship, most likely begun through Donne's introduction of the two men in about 1624—that is, the year when Donne took up his appointment as rector of St. Dunstan's-in-the-West, Walton's parish church. Walton intended his *Life* as a preface to the *Reliquiae Wottonianae* (entered in the Stationers' Register for 3 November 1648 but not published until 1651), beginning his account with a characteristic apology for his boldness. If only some one of his many surviving friends "*of higher parts and imployment, had been pleas'd to have commended*" him to posterity, then Walton would not have come forward; yet "*gratitude to the memory of my dead friend*" and a number of requests "*have had a power to perswade me to undertake*" the *Life*. Walton is "*modestly confident*" that his "*humble lan-*

guage shall be accepted, because I shall present all Readers with a Commixture of truth, and Sir Henry Wotton'*s merits*" (*Lives*, 97–98). The final statement of the *Life* reiterates this sentiment: "*All Readers are requested to believe, that he was worthy of a more worthy Pen, to have preserved his* Memory, *and commended his* Merits *to the imitation of Posterity*" (*Lives*, 151).

Walton's *Life of Wotton* is testimony to a warm and fraternal relationship, evidently heightened by a common love for angling. In *The Compleat Angler*, which was first published in 1653, only two years after the *Life of Wotton*, Walton, in order to recommend "the lawfulness of fishing," offers examples of notable men devoted to this gentle "Art of Angling." One person of exceptional wisdom, highly esteemed by all the world, is Sir Henry Wotton, of whom Walton offers a brief and affectionate sketch. Walton calls him "that under-valuer of mony . . . (a man with whom I have often fish'd and convers'd)" and

> a man whose forraign imployments in the service of this Nation, and whose experience, learning, wit and cheerfulness, made his company to be esteemed one of the delights of mankind; this man, whose very approbation of Angling were sufficient to convince any modest Censurer of it, this man was also a most dear lover, and a frequent practicer of the Art of Angling; of which he would say, *'Twas an imployment for his idle time, which was then not idly spent;* for Angling was after tedious study *A rest to his mind, a cheerer of his spirits, a diversion of sadness, a calmer of unquiet thoughts, a Moderator of passions, a procurer of contentedness, and that it begot habits of peace and patience in those that profest and practic'd it.* . . . This was the saying of that Learned man; and I do easily believe that peace, and patience, and a calm content did cohabit in the cheerful heart of Sir *Henry Wotton.*[9]

Of all Walton's biographies, the *Life of Sir Henry Wotton* is the most entertaining, amiable, and witty. Walton always writes of persons he likes and admires, but in this instance he is looking with special regard at a fellow enthusiast of angling; he writes of Wotton as an urbane friend who possesses the worthiest virtues in a lively and well-stocked mind. Walton seems relaxed in this presentation of his friend, for he aims principally to represent an illustrious life, not to exalt it, as in his near canonization of Donne, nor to urge (or imply) wide-ranging moral principles, doctrines, or beliefs. Wotton's biographer is certainly well disposed, and he cleverly selects amusing anecdotes for telling the life story; but he is generally more detached and objective in the *Life of Wotton* than elsewhere, finding in this subject one who might match his own irenicism and dislike of contention and divisive argument. Here Walton is most relaxed, working in the same spirit as that of *The Compleat Angler*.

Walton is highly selective in the details that he gives about Wotton's life, and one feels that he must be relating only the tiniest part of what he knows. The *Life* is very broadly sketched, giving an impression of a worldly man whose adventures lead at last to final years of genial retirement and contemplation. After a lively account of his distinguished ancestry, including an amusing description of his father's second marriage, we are told of his education and care at home in Bocton Hall in Kent. When the time was right, he was sent to Winchester School, that "he might in his youth be moulded into a Method of living by Rule, which his wise Father knew to be the most necessary way, to make the future part of his life, both happy to himself, and useful for discharge of all business, whether publick or private" (*Lives*, 99).

From Winchester, Wotton went in 1584, at age 16, to New College, Oxford, with which his school was connected through their common founder, William Wickham, sometime bishop of Winchester. After a short time at New College, Wotton moved first to Hart Hall, where he met the youthful John Donne, then to Queen's, where he wrote a play entitled *Tancredo*, which has not survived, based on Tasso's *Gerusalemme Liberata* (first published in 1581). Walton reminds us somewhat later in the *Life* that the friendship of Wotton and Donne began at this time (*Lives*, 106), a point that must have seemed important to him—though he introduces it awkwardly as a kind of afterthought. Walton wishes to show that Wotton's play demonstrated ingenuity beyond the years of its author, for it was "so interwoven with Sentences, and for the Method and exact personating those humours, passions, and dispositions, which he proposed to represent, so performed, that the gravest of that society [of Queen's] declared, he had in a sleight imployment, given an early and a solid testimony of his future abilities" (*Lives*, 100). Walton's reminiscence provides a useful example of his technique of interpreting and directing the future through the past.

Walton passes on to the lectures that Wotton gave as a master of arts, three presentations *De Oculo*, on the question "*Whether we see by the Emission of the Beams from within, or Reception of the Species from without?*" (*Lives*, 100). The lectures excited the admiration of the learned Alberico Gentili, an Italian protestant refugee who became professor of Civil Law in Oxford, and provided the beginning of Wotton's long association with Continental, particularly Italian, men of letters: Sir Henry possessed already "a propensity and connaturalness to the *Italian* Language, and

those Studies whereof *Gentilis* was a great Master," so that their friendship daily increased. Now Walton, having digressed to describe the death
of Wotton's father, leads his subject to foreign travel—a nine-year journey through France, Germany, and Italy, from which at the age of about
30 he returned with his wit polished and his conversation and knowledge
improved. Walton writes of him at this time as one "noted by many, both
for his Person and Comportment; for indeed he was of a choice shape, tall
of stature, and of a most perswasive behaviour; which was so mixed with
sweet Discourse, and Civilities, as gained him much love from all Persons
with whom he entred into an acquaintance" (*Lives*, 107).[10] One such person was the earl of Essex, in whose service Wotton was joined; with him,
and with other rising courtiers, including Donne, he sailed on the famous
expedition to Cadiz in 1596 and to the Azores in the following year. The
voyage to Ireland in 1599 was not successful, for this led to Essex's
downfall, and to Wotton's hurried departure for the Continent. In all of
these adventures, Walton gives to Wotton's life a radiance, and a character of immeasurable probity. Wotton would seem to have lived his
youth—and all of his years—in a certain pious blamelessness.

How Wotton came in disguise to warn the Scottish King James VI of
the plot against his life, how James, as soon as he became king also of
England, sent for Wotton and appointed him ambassador to Venice, and
how Wotton advanced the Protestant cause there against the papacy
Walton relates in a delightful series of anecdotes. He pauses over Wotton's one misadventure, his defining in some correspondence that came
to the king's attention how an ambassador might pleasantly be defined
as "*Legatus est vir bonus peregrè missus ad mentiendum Reipublicæ causâ,*" that
is, "*An Embassadour is an honest man, sent to* lie *abroad for the good of his
Country*" (*Lives*, 121), a pun being intended on "lie." The wittiness
explained, Wotton becomes even more highly regarded by the king.
Walton brings his account forward, moving Wotton back to England in
the last year of James's reign, quite full of debts, "he being always so
careless of money, as though our Saviours words, *Care not for to morrow*,
were to be literally understood. . . . And Sir *Henry* who had for many
years (like *Sisyphus*) rolled the restless stone of a State-imployment;
knowing experimentally, that the great blessing of sweet content was
not to be found in multitudes of men or business: and, that a *Colledge*
was the fittest place to nourish *holy thoughts*, and to afford rest both to
his body and mind, which his age (being now almost threescore years)
seemed to require, did therefore use his own, and the interest of all his
friends to procure that place" (*Lives*, 127–28). "That place" of course

was Eton College, where Wotton would pass his final years as provost (1624–1639), "being made *Deacon* with all convenient speed" (*Lives*, 129). Yet this new employment is seen as the culmination of a busy life, certainly not as a point of decline.

We should remember that Walton had similarly brought Donne to a point of new beginning: Donne was 43 when he entered holy orders, and he would live for 16 years; Wotton was 56 when he was ordained deacon, and he would live for 15 years. The correspondence of the two men is close in Walton's mind. Wotton's life change is treated as a conversion, and if not as dramatic as Donne's it is nevertheless described as the outstanding highlight of a distinguished career. We are told that an old friend meets Sir Henry Wotton shortly after his ordination; he is now wearing a surplice, and the friend "joyed him of his new habit," which brought the reply

> I thank God *and the* King, *by whose goodness I now am in this condition; a condition, which that Emperor* Charles *the Fifth seem'd to approve: who, after so many remarkable Victories, when his glory was great in the eyes of all men, freely gave up his* Crown, *and the many cares that attended it, to* Philip *his Son, making a holy retreat to a Cloysteral life, where he might by devout* meditations *consult with* God (which the rich or busie men seldom do) *and have leisure both to examine the errors of his life past, and prepare for that great day, wherein all flesh must make an account of their actions: And after a kind of tempestuous life, I now have the like advantage from him,* that makes the out-goings of the morning to praise him; *even from my* God, *whom I daily magnifie for this particular mercy, of an exemption from business, a quiet mind, and a liberal maintenance, even in this part of my life, when my* age *and* infirmities *seem to sound me a retreat from the pleasures of this world, and invite me to contemplation, in which I have ever taken the greatest felicity.* (*Lives*, 129–30)

Walton thus imagines the speech, which may bear some connection to words actually spoken; but typically he provides the turn of phrase and the emphasis. Moreover, Walton interprets the occasion and the speech according to the structural needs of his narrative.

Walton mentions Donne only twice in his *Life of Wotton*, first, as we have seen, as the friend of Wotton at Hart Hall, Oxford; and second as the author of a verse letter to Sir Henry "at his going Ambassador to Venice," which Walton gives in full (*Lives*, 114–15).[11] Yet the fortunes of Wotton and Donne are closely connected, which Walton obliquely acknowledges through the many implicit parallels between the two *Lives*. There are broad similarities, such as the early reputation for learning in each of the *Lives;* the importance of King James, with his disfavor, followed by his approval; reference to pecuniary distress in each; Donne's indiscretion through his sudden marriage and Wotton's unfortunate connection with Essex. Parallels are evident in small details, too, including such examples as the point that Donne and Wotton become deacons with all convenient speed; in each, the holy retirement of the emperor Charles V is cited, and also King James's motto (*Beati pacifici*); and there is offered moral advice from the deathbed. Walton seems, indeed, to have composed the later *Life of Wotton* with the earlier one of Donne very much in his mind.[12]

Walton established his general scheme for writing biography in his *Life of Donne*, and he follows it in all of the subsequent *Lives:* an early, energetic, secular life; a turning point, climax, or crisis; a later, more contemplative, highly focused life; a "holy death." Characters are displayed through imagined dialogue, lively anecdotes, interpretive comments; thematic consistency is provided by a steadily conservative, cautious point of view; and moral instruction is offered along with entertainment. With the success of his *Life of Donne*, Walton would have seen no need to change this ideal formula, and he was able also to invest Wotton's *Life* with the kinds of details that obviously linked it with *Donne*. Probably Walton saw Donne and Walton as having parallel lives, the one interpreting or speaking to the other, even as the two were united in friendship. Certainly he would not have anticipated in 1651 that he might turn again to biography—he would occupy himself with his own "autobiography" in *The Compleat Angler* (1653), into which he fits not only himself but also such friends as Donne and Wotton. Walton quite honestly tells the reader in his last collection of *Lives* (now including Hooker, Herbert, and Sanderson) that he wrote the first two lives with no plans for more: *"Having writ these two lives; I lay quiet twenty years, without a thought of either troubling my self or others, by any new ingagement in this kind, for I thought I knew my unfitness"* (*Lives*, 5). But the demands of Walton's friends and the circumstances of the Restoration church forced a change of mind.

Walton may have continued to meditate on his writings during this long period, however, for the Restoration editions of works he had already composed reveal many changes, both great and small. Almost nothing that Walton wrote remained unrevised, and his principal works seem always to have been in progress. A single passage from the *Life of Wotton* well illustrates Walton's continuous composition, and it should serve to characterize the scrupulous, even nervous care of an author never quite satisfied with his work.

Five editions of *Wotton* appeared during Walton's lifetime (1651, 1654, 1670, 1672, 1675), and only the last, published when Walton was 82, shows little if any authorial intervention. The second and third editions appeared, as both of their title pages declare, "with large additions"; the edition of 1670 is even longer, and compared with the first edition, it is increased in length by at least one-sixth. In the passage cited here, we are reminded of Wotton's important ambassadorship to Venice. The background of the incident recalls James's policy of bringing together a league of Protestant states to oppose Catholic Spain. Accordingly, Wotton plotted to introduce Protestantism into Italy by starting with Venice; there he celebrated English religious rites, in his own private chapel, which many Venetians attended. The decidedly independent Venetian government was, in part through these events, happy to annoy Pope Clement VIII, who may have wished to avoid a struggle. But his successor strongly asserted the privileges of the Church of Rome; thus the election of Pope Paul V in 1605 led to a more telling conflict, which the secular Venetian state saw as a fight against papal aggression. Walton writes of this situation in his first edition, which appeared with *Reliquiae Wottonianae* (1651):

> The justice, or injustice of such power, used by the *Venetians*, had some calm debates betwixt Pope *Clement* the 8, and that *Republick*. But *Clement* dying, Pope *Paul* the fifth (who succeeded him) brought it to an high contention with the *Venetians;* objecting those acts of that State to be a diminution of his just Power, and limited a time for their revocation; threatning, if he were not obeyed, to proceed to Excommunication of the *Republick;* who offered to shew both reason and ancient custome to warrant their Actions. But this *Pope*, contrary to his Predecessors, required absolute obedience without disputes. Thus it continued for about a yeer, the Pope threatning Excommunication, and the *Venetians* still answering him with fair speeches, and no performance: At last, the Pope did excommunicate the *Duke;* whole *Senate*, and all their Dominions; then he shut up all the *Churches*, charging the whole *Clergie* to forbear all sacred offices to any of the *Venetians*, till their obedience should make them capable of absolution. (sig. b12ᵛ)

Although the second edition of 1654 is similar to the first edition, Walton makes a number of alterations, which are characteristic of the extraordinary trouble and often tedious worry he expended over his composition:

> The justice, or injustice of such power, then used by the *Venetians*, had formerly had some calm debates betwixt Pope *Clement* the Eighth, and that *Republick:* But, *Clement* dying, Pope *Paul* the Fifth (who succeeded him) being of another temper, brought it to an high contention with the *Venetians;* objecting those acts of that State, to be a diminution of his just power; and limited a time for their revocation; threatning, if he were not obeyed, to proceed to excommunication of the *Republick;* who still offered to shew both reason and ancient custome to warrant their Actions. But this *Pope* contrary to his Predecessors moderation, required absolute obedience without disputes.
>
> Thus it continued for about a year; the Pope still threatning Excommunication, and the *Venetians* still answering him with fair speeches, and no performance, till at last the *Pope* did excommunicate the *Duke*, the whole *Senate*, and all their Dominions, and then shut up all their *Churches*, charging the whole Clergie, to forbear all sacred Offices to the *Venetians*, till their Obedience should render him capable of *absolution*. (40–41)

Walton introduces "formerly" in the first sentence and also the important phrase "being of another temper"; "who offered" becomes "who still offered." In the next sentence, "his Predecessors" is modified by "his Predecessors moderation." The long paragraph is now divided into two paragraphs, and the "Pope threatning excommunication" is now "still threatning . . . till at last," with the series slightly revised to emphasize its parallel elements. Finally, the concluding phrase ends more significantly, for "their obedience should make them capable of absolution" becomes "their Obedience should render him capable of *absolution*," the direction and the quality of the absolution now being changed, an alteration that Walton rejects in the subsequent revisions, as we shall see.

The 1670 edition of the *Life of Wotton* much expands this passage, with vital consequences:

> The justice, or injustice of such power, then used by the *Venetians*, had formerly had some calm debates betwixt the present Pope *Clement* the Eighth, and that *Republick:* for he did not excommunicate them; considering (as I conceive) that in the late *Council of Trent* it was at last (after many Politique disturbances, and delayes, and indeavours to preserve the Popes present power) declar'd, in order to a general reformation of those many Errours which were in time crept into the Church: that though

Discipline, and especial *Excommunication* be one of the chief sinews of Church government; and intended to keep men in obedience to it: for which end, it was declar'd to be very profitable; yet it was also declar'd, and advised to be used with great sobriety and care: because experience had informed them, that when it was pronounced unadvisedly or rashly, it became more *contemn'd* then *fear'd*. And, though this was the advice of that Council at the Conclusion of it, which was not many years before this quarrel with the *Venetians:* yet this prudent, patient Pope *Clement* dying: *Pope Paul* the fift, who succeeded him, being a man of a much hotter temper, brought this difference with the *Venetians* to a much higher Contention: objecting those late acts of that State, to be a diminution of his just power, and limited a time for their revocation; threatning, if he were not obeyed, to proceed to excommunication of the *Republick;* who still offered to shew both reason and ancient custom to warrant their Actions. But this *Pope*, contrary to his Predecessors moderation, required absolute obedience without disputes.

Thus it continued for about a year; the Pope still threatning Excommunication, and the *Venetians* still answering him with fair speeches, and no performance, till at last, the Popes zeal to the *Apostolick Sea*, did make him to excommunicate the *Duke*, the whole *Senate*, and all their Dominions; and then shut up all their *Churches;* charging the whole Clergy to forbear all sacred Offices to the *Venetians*, till their Obedience should render them capable of *Absolution*. (33–35)

Walton provides further historical background, which he interprets with obvious prejudice. The Council of Trent aimed to correct errors in the church yet affirmed its power of excommunication "to keep men in obedience to it." Pope Clement becomes "prudent" and "patient," his successor "being a man of a much hotter temper" (not simply, as described earlier, of "another temper"), who lacks moderation and possesses "zeal to the *Apostolick Sea*." Walton is still not quite content with these changes, for in the next and fourth revision of 1672, which was reissued in 1675 and is the basis of all subsequent editions, he emphasizes "calm debates" early in the first sentence with a repetition of "I say, calm" (sig. c3v). Walton is also more particular about time, for he tells us that Paul succeeded Clement "though not immediately, yet in the same year"; and the period allowed for the revocation of the Venetian state's powers is limited to "twenty four dayes." Having adjusted these details, Walton may have been finally satisfied with this *Life*. Walton has not only filled out the historical circumstances of his original description but also has taken a more sharply defined position that asserts the rights of the state.

These rights Walton may have wished to identify with his own strong monarchical disposition, easier to maintain in the Restoration than during the Interregnum. He was evidently discovering the voice through which he would articulate the claims of royalism and episcopacy in an English setting. These attitudes become notably clear in his approach to the later lives of Hooker, Herbert, and especially Sanderson.

Chapter Three

Walton the Biographer:
Hooker, Herbert, and Sanderson

The Life of Mr. Richard Hooker

Although Walton continued to work on and refine his earliest *Lives* and especially *The Compleat Angler* during the years of the Interregnum, he seems to have had no plans for beginning any new writing project. When Laud died in 1645, the established church officially disappeared, and its clergy dispossessed and scattered. In establishing its ascendancy, Parliament abolished the Book of Common Prayer. Many clergy continued, though illegally, in familiar ways; many more sought some quiet refuge in the countryside, and still others traveled to the Continent. When Charles II returned to England in May 1660, Walton and his friends celebrated the restoration not only of the monarchy but also of the episcopacy. Those bishops and other clergy who managed to remain faithful to the old regime returned with increased influence and importance. The old Laudians recovered their positions, and a younger generation of dependable adherents sought preferment. John Cosin, for example, the ousted dean of Peterborough (and master of Peterhouse, Cambridge), who conducted services for the exiled English court in Paris, was quickly appointed to the wealthy see of Durham. William Juxon, who received Charles's last words on the scaffold on 30 January 1649, was promoted from bishop of London to archbishop of Canterbury, and Gilbert Sheldon succeeded Juxon in London and also, at Juxon's death (in 1663), as archbishop. Meanwhile, George Morley was nominated to Worcester and later was translated to Winchester. Walton counted Sheldon and Morley among his friends—indeed, he lived in Morley's household during most of the last 20 years of his life.

John Gauden, another of the old clergy, was an ambitious and temporizing person who aimed to ingratiate himself with such powerful men as Sheldon, and he did in fact receive the bishopric of Exeter, a poor and indebted see, which he despised. Gauden continued his efforts to gain recognition and favor, and to this end he undertook to edit and publish the works of Richard Hooker, who died in 1600, accompanied by a biographical account of the famous apologist. Hooker, it must be remembered, was regarded as a father of the church, an undoubted champion of the Reformed faith, a steadfast opponent of nonconformists, and a sure upholder of the royal prerogative and of the episcopacy. The High Church party—the intellectual descendants of Laud— were pleased to trace their genealogy from Hooker, and his reputation as their preeminent theologian seemed incontestable. Yet knowledge of Hooker's writing was generally based on the first five books of his *Ecclesiastical Polity;* the preface and books 1 through 4 were published in 1593, and book 5, which exceeded in length all that preceded it, appeared in 1597. Hooker had planned three more books, but he died in 1600, before seeing them "perfected" and into print. Without these last books of the *Polity,* Hooker's full argument is truncated, for in them, and especially in books 7 and 8, he planned a detailed discussion of the doctrine of the church and the nature of the episcopacy (in book 7), and an account of the royal supremacy and its relationship to the church (in book 8): jurisdiction is the theme of these three posthumous books, whether by lay elders (book 6), by the bishops (book 7), or by the monarchy (book 8). His manuscripts for these last books were alleged to have been stolen, or mangled, or even destroyed immediately after his death. Yet a small portion of book 6 and some chapters of book 8 circulated in manuscript for almost 50 years; these materials did not appear in print until 1648, however, in an edition apparently sponsored by James Ussher, archbishop of Armagh. But book 7, on the episcopacy, did not circulate, was apparently unknown, and appeared for the first time in Gauden's edition of 1662.

How Gauden came to be entrusted with an edition of Hooker, including the important seventh book, is by no means clear. He had claimed authorship of the *Eikon Basilike,* which had been ascribed to Charles I, and probably as part of his campaign to advance to a wealthier diocese—he hoped for Winchester—he wished to curry more favor with Sheldon, who would soon become archbishop of Canterbury, and with the king himself. Gauden seems to have undertaken this new edition of Hooker's *Works* largely on his own initiative, adding book 7 of the *Ecclesiastical Polity,* which he seems to have received from Sheldon's safekeeping. The edition is thus expanded, "to which," Gauden writes in his preface, "by the care of some Learned men, especially of the Right Reverend Father in God, *Gilbert* now Lord Bishop of *London,* those gen-

uine additions are now made of the *three last Books*, promised and performed by him [that is, Hooker], but long concealed from publique
view, not without great injury to the publique good."[1]

Gauden dedicated the edition, accompanied by his "Life of Hooker,"
to the king on 1 January 1661, according to the *engraved* title page—
the work was obviously intended to be a New Year's present—though
the *printed* title page gives the date as 1662. The "Life" is separately
paginated (though not separately signed), and book 7 is separately paginated and signed, for certainly it was set in type and added after the
book was ready to be printed. One may presume that book 7 came to
light during the year between the two dates of the edition and that it
was hastily composed, inserted, and bound into the waiting copies.
These details about the transmission of Hooker's *Ecclesiastical Polity*, and
especially book 7, which must have been suppressed until 1662, are cru-
cial to our understanding of Walton's *Life of Hooker;* for Walton is react-
ing to Gauden's "Life" in order to provide an official view of Hooker—
that same Hooker whose convictions, as we shall see, in fact do not
unequivocally support the Restoration and High Church understanding
of the episcopacy. Walton explains how he came to be involved in cor-
recting Gauden's errors. Having lain "quiet twenty years" without further biographical writing, he declares:

> *Dr.* Gauden (*then Lord Bishop of* Exeter) *publisht* the Life of Mr. Richard
> Hooker, (*so he called it*) *with so many dangerous mistakes, both of him and his*
> Books, *that discoursing of them with his* Grace, Gilbert *that now is Lord*
> *Archbishop of* Canterbury; *he injoined me to examine some Circumstances, and*
> *then rectifie the Bishops mistakes, by giving the World a fuller and a truer account*
> *of* Mr. Hooker *and his* Books, *then that Bishop had done, and, I know I have*
> *done so. And, let me tell the Reader, that till his Grace had laid this injunction*
> *upon me, I could not admit a thought of any fitness in me to undertake it: but,*
> *when he had twice injoin'd me to it, I then declin'd my own, and trusted his judg-*
> *ment, and submitted to his Commands: concluding, that if I did not, I could not*
> *forbear accusing my self of disobedience....* Thus I became ingaged into the
> third Life. (*Lives,* 5–6)

We need to examine Gauden's "Life" in order to gain some idea of what
Walton set out to remedy.

Gauden's "Life" begins with an extended account of the Elizabethan
church of Hooker's time, with a register of events down through the
Interregnum and to the Restoration. Gauden oddly suggests that
Hooker was partly responsible for not entirely rooting out the noncon-

formists when he might supposedly have had the chance. He concludes
an early section of his "Life":

> These principles of Christian *hopes*, no *times*, no *Tyrants*, or *Tragedies*, were
> able to banish out of good mens mindes: And blessed be God, we have
> not onely lived to see and feel the predictions of this great Prophet
> [Hooker] fulfilled; but we have *outlived their dreadful accomplishments*, and
> after the *earthquake, tempest* and *fire* are past, we have heard the *soft voyce of*
> *Gods presence;* we are come to that *serenity* and safety, as may dare to own
> the sin and shame of former times and actions; to weep over our past
> calamities, and to joy in present mercies. . . . We have now *liberty*, not
> onely to *read*, but *reprint* and practice Mr. *Hookers* Ecclesiastical Polity; to
> which, as to *Jeremies Prophesie*, many more like words *are now added*,
> together with some larger *Commentary* upon his life and death: All which
> may be both pleasant and profitable to the *present age, restored now* (as the
> *dispossessed Demoniac*) to its *right wits* and *estates;* to its *former laws*, and true
> liberties in *Church* and *State*. (Gauden, 6 [Cv])

Gauden's prolixity is irritating, and his description of Hooker's life is eva-
sive, inaccurate, and often unflattering. Hooker's parents are described as
honest, industrious, and healthy—blessings they conferred on their children. Richard Hooker is described as an average though diligent student
in the grammar school of Exeter; he had few friends, and "his natural
temper was slow and reserved." At Corpus Christi College, Oxford, he
continued to lead a retired life: "He was so locked up and reserved by a
natural modesty, and *self-deficiency* or distrust, that he seemed to think it
reward sufficient to have the conscience of well-doing; and *pleasure*
enough, to see himself daily profit in his studies" (Gauden, 10 [Dv]).

The portrait is hardly complimentary, nor does it readily anticipate
the hero we will meet in Walton's *Life*. Gauden continues: "Yet while he
lived in the *Colledge* and *University*, there seems to have been no *great*
notice of him, further then of a good *plodding Student*, one that *lay heavy*
on the plow, and was *daily sowing* good seed, but few expected so rich *an*
harvest as afterward grew up in his soul, and was reaped by *his pen:* He
was like a *rich mine* not yet fully discovered, but daily improving upon
the Explorators" (Gauden, 10 [Dv]). Gauden now describes Hooker's
priestly vocation and his appointments to humble and insignificant rural
parishes: "Mr. *Hooker* looked more to his employment and retirement
then his *Preferment:* hence I finde him *aground* as soon as *lanched* out, and
as it were buried so soon as he parted from his *Mother the University*, still
shut up for many years in *Countrey obscurities*, where there could be no

great profit nor pleasure, onely he fancied this way of living . . . out of the *crowd, noise* and *tintamar* of the *great World*, chusing a little *Creek*, rather then a great *arm* of the *Sea* to anchor in; where, as there is more water, so there are greater winds and waves" (Gauden, 13 [Er]). At considerable length, Gauden summarizes the different books of Hooker's *Ecclesiastical Polity*, though its occasion is left vague and its value inadequately understood.

Gauden next turns to Hooker's preaching at the Temple in the Inns of Court, and his contention with Walter Travers—not connecting this part of his life with the *Ecclesiastical Polity*. He compares Travers's preaching with Hooker's to the latter's disadvantage. Although Hooker was more thoughtful and worthier than his adversary, he was less impressive:

> Mr. *Hooker* was a *deeper*, but *silenter stream;* running, as more slowly and quietly, so with some *obscurity* and *dulness* to common Auditors; so confident of the sacred power and efficacy of the matter he delivered, that he thought it needed no great setting off: This made him so far from *any life* in his looks, gestures or pronunciations, that he preached like *a living*, but scarce *moving statue:* His eyes *stedfastly* fixed on the same place from the beginning to the end of his *Sermons;* his *body* unmoved, his *tone* much to an *Unisone*, and very *unemphatick;* so variously doth God distribute *his gifts*, not *lading* all *in one* bottom. (Gauden, 30 [gv])

Travers had "the *broader sails*, the fairer *waistcloaths*, and *larger streams.*" Both are silenced, Gauden says, when the contention grows too hot; but he fails to notice that Archbishop Whitgift deprived Travers alone of his position. Similarly misleading is Gauden's account of Hooker's death, "with less incumbrance and care, having neither wife, nor childe, nor any kindred, whose eyes had failed for his charity till his death; he rather prevented them, and as he could spare it, spent it, not in Epicurism and Luxury, but in such a frugal *decency* as best became him, his relations, his neighbours, and the poor" (Gauden, 35–36 [g4r-v]). Gauden quite evidently was unaware that Hooker was married, with children.

Gauden begins to draw his "Life" to its end, for some four folio pages remain in which he informs us about Hooker's death and the honors accorded to his memory. Now we have a summary of Hooker's character, much in the tone of what has preceded:

> His diet, as his apparel, plain, but decent: His entertainments hospitable, but Philosophical, yea Theological: His recreation, as to expensiveness,

none; for he took pleasure in nothing so much as that by which he prof-
ited most, in *study* or *discourse;* He lived daily as in the *Confines of Heaven*,
and *next door to Death*, which is the *porch of Eternity:* He never had the lev-
ity of youth, much less the lubricity, being grave and good betimes; nor
did he grow morose, or tetrical, or covetous, or ambitious, or proud with
years, though crowned with the *garlands* of Applause, and the *lawrels* of
great Learning, yea with the *fruits* of noble and excellent *Works:* His humble soul was as a fruitful field, nothing elevated, when most enriched; or as
the heavenly lights, satisfied with shining to others. (Gauden, 36 [g4v])

Gauden's account of Hooker's "Holy Life, and Happy Death" leaves us
with the impression of a learned yet dull man, and we may wonder
whether we should trouble to read his *Works*. I have quoted at length
from Gauden in order to display what Walton was writing against, for
Walton's *Life* indeed elevates Hooker to the position in which the
Restoration church wished to see him: the greatest "doctor" of the English Reformation, a systematic theologian of firm belief and unwavering devotion to the *Ecclesia Anglicana*.

Walton accomplishes several general ends. He begins by establishing
his own credibility, describing his sources and their accuracy and close-
ness to Hooker; for Walton confesses that of course he *"knew him not in
his Life, and must therefore not only look back to his Death, now 64 years past;
but almost 50 years beyond that, even to his Childhood"* (*Lives*, 159). But he
tells us that he knew William Cranmer, grandnephew of the great archbishop (Walton's first wife, Rachel, was a sister of William's), who was
associated with Hooker at Corpus Christi, Oxford; William Cranmer's
brother, George, was a pupil of Hooker's. A second Cranmer sister was
married to John Spenser, who was president of Hooker's college.
William Cranmer and his two sisters are said to have had some of their
education with Hooker in his house when he was the priest of Bishopsbourne, near Canterbury. Walton later learned much about Hooker
from them; he tells of his friendship with Archbishop James Ussher,
who knew Hooker (and collected his manuscripts); with Thomas Morton, bishop of Durham; and with John Hales and others who were connected to Hooker or who had some knowledge *"of his Person, his Nature,
the management of his Time, his Wife, his Family and the Fortune of him and
his"* (*Lives*, 161). Walton is at some pains in his *Life of Hooker* to give
dates and particular details of a kind that are less common in the other
Lives, for his purpose here is partly to correct false information.

Walton's design is not only to rectify Gauden's errors but also to ele-
vate Hooker's character while casting doubt on the authenticity of the

last three books of the *Ecclesiastical Polity*. Gauden had assumed that these books were genuine, and the copy he received of book 7 seemed to prove the case beyond doubt:

> The Venerable *Author of these eight Books*, had formerly given the world an account of *his design in each of them:* Of which, five have many year been *extant in publique;* the last three were thought to have been *never finished*, and to be sure, they have been for many ages *suppressed;* which are now come to light, after our late long troubles. . . . Such as they are, it is thought meet to present them to the *Reader;* each of them is by *learned Criticks* judged to be *genuine*, or *Authentick*, though possibly not so compleat and exact as the curious Author intended: The seventh book, by comparing the writing of it with *other indisputable Papers*, or known *Manuscripts* of Mr. *Hookers*, is undoubtedly his *own hand* throughout: The eighth is written by *another hand* (as a Copy) but interlined in many places with Mr. *Hookers own characters*, as owned by him. (Gauden, 26 [F5v])

Gauden is almost certainly telling the truth, for his testimony firmly accords with my own study of the last books, and although the manuscript of the seventh book that Gauden caused to be printed has been lost, the resulting text shows evidence of having been set from Hooker's own holograph.[2] Gauden himself was a moderate churchman with an outlook similar to that of Archbishop Ussher, and he might have been happy to discover that Hooker was much more yielding on the question of the historic episcopacy than most of the High Churchmen who claimed, or who wished to claim, descendancy from him. Hooker writes:

> Bishops albeit they may avouch with conformity of truth, that their Authority hath thus descended even from the very Apostles themselves, yet the absolute and everlasting continuance of it, they cannot say that any Commandment of the Lord doth injoyn; And therefore must acknowledge that the Church hath power by universal consent upon urgent cause to take it away, if thereunto she be constrained through the proud, tyrannical, and unreformable dealings of her Bishops, whose Regiment she hath thus long delighted in, because she hath found it good and requisite to be so governed. Wherefore least Bishops forget themselves, as if none on earth had Authority to touch their states, let them continually bear in mind, that it is rather the force of custome, whereby the Church having so long found it good to continue under the Regiment of her vertuous Bishop, doth still uphold, maintain, and honour them in that respect, then that any such true and heavenly Law can be showed,

by the evidence whereof it may of a truth appear that the Lord himself
hath appointed Presbyters for ever to be under the Regiment of Bishops,
in what sort soever they behave themselves; let this consideration be a
bridle unto them, let it teach them not to disdain the advice of their Presbyters, but to use their authority with so much the greater humility and
moderation, as a Sword which the Church hath power to take from
them.[3]

Hooker has much more to say along these lines—the discourse is difficult and often ambivalent, but the principal implication of his message
is clear: the episcopacy is traditional, often useful, but not essential to
the essence (the *esse*), or being, of the church. Hooker does not argue for
the divine establishment of the episcopacy; he speaks much more cau-
tiously on this issue than his High Church successors would have
wished. Walton, in his turn, casts doubt on Hooker's authorship, and he
does his best to make Hooker speak as the bishops wanted him to sound
and to take positions with which they might have agreed.

Walton arranges his *Life of Hooker* in a way that is reminiscent of his
earlier biographies: description of the early preparatory years that lead
to a turning point, then on to maturity, the last years filled with accomplishment, wisdom, and honor, and at the end a holy and memorable
death. Where Walton's information is sparse, particularly about
Hooker's youth, he provides general information about the times and
the age, or else he associates Hooker with eminent figures. In the opening paragraph, for example, Walton tells us that Hooker was born at
Heavitree, near Exeter, the birthplace also of Sir Thomas Bodley. And
the county of Devon is the birthplace of such men as Bishop Jewel, Sir
Francis Drake, Sir Walter Raleigh, and others who would, like Richard
Hooker, become known for their "valor and learning." Again, Walton
cleverly uses this kind of laudable association when he brings Hooker to
Corpus Christi (one of the new Elizabethan foundations), with the pre-
cise date of admission, in his 19th year, on 24 December 1573, remarking that the college had already Jewell, John Reynolds, Thomas Jack-
son, and others in its fellowship. Walton records that Sir Henry Savile,
the learned editor of St. John Chrysostom and provost of Eton, "had the
happiness to be a Contemporary, and familiar friend to Mr. *Hooker*," and
adds, "[L]et Posterity know it" (*Lives*, 171). Thus, while we may know
little of Hooker himself, we can at least infer a good character from the
quality of his friends, or from the names that ought to be connected
with his.

As if to impugn Gauden's review of the church and its quarrels, Walton provides a long interlude on the "discontents and dangers" of the Elizabethan church that Hooker would come to address, and Walton includes a long account of Archbishop Whitgift, Hooker's eventual patron. Hooker had earlier come to the attention of the archbishop of York, Edwin Sandys; for Hooker was tutor to the younger Sandys (and George Cranmer), and the archbishop saw that he was preferred to the mastership of the Temple. This selection was timely, we are told, for it saved Hooker from the tedium of a country parsonage, Drayton Beauchamp in Buckinghamshire, where he had settled with his new wife, Joan Churchman, in 1584.

No figure in Walton receives such disparaging treatment as Joan Churchman, but Walton's depiction of her is part of a broader purpose, which is to celebrate Hooker and his "true" life's work in the *Ecclesiastical Polity*. With this purpose in mind, Walton gives us one of his most vivid scenes. He records that while still at Corpus Christi, Hooker, recently ordained deacon and priest, was appointed on one occasion to preach at St. Paul's in London. After a difficult journey to London, he arrived at the house of John Churchman in a wet and pitiful condition, but Mrs. Churchman provided for him such "diligent attendance" that he was later able to perform the office and preach his sermon. Now the grateful Hooker thought himself bound to the Churchmans, listening to everything Mrs. Churchman said "so that the good man came to be perswaded by her, *that he was a man of a tender constitution*, and *that it was best for him to have a Wife, that might prove a Nurse to him;* such an one as *might both prolong his life, and make it more comfortable; and such a one she could and would provide for him, if he thought fit to marry*" (*Lives*, 177). The "one" proved to be her daughter Joan, "who brought him neither Beauty nor Portion. . . . And by this marriage the good man was drawn from the tranquillity of his Colledge, from that Garden of Piety, of Pleasure, of Peace, and a sweet Conversation, into the thorny Wilderness of a busie World; into those corroding cares that attend a married Priest" (*Lives*, 178–79). When his two pupils Edwin Sandys and George Cranmer journeyed to see him at Drayton Beauchamp,

> They found him with a Book in his hand (it was the *Odes* of *Horace*) he being then like humble and innocent *Abel*, tending his small allotment of sheep in a common field, which he told his Pupils he was forced to do then, for that his servant was gone home to Dine, and assist his Wife to do some necessary houshold business. But when his servant returned and

released him, then his two Pupils attended him unto his house, where their best entertainment was his quiet company, which was presently denied them: for, *Richard was call'd to rock the Cradle;* and the rest of their welcom was so like this, that they staid but till next morning, which was time enough to discover and pity their Tutors condition. (*Lives*, 179)

Walton's view of Hooker's domestic circumstances, an unusually detailed and forthright scene for the literature of this period, is carefully calculated to cast Joan in the worst possible light so that we may believe she might be capable of any outrage—even the destruction of Hooker's manuscripts.

From this unhappy situation, Hooker is rescued, only to be put into the theological turmoil of the Temple, a situation that Walton broadly surveys. The controversy that ensued between the Presbyterian Travers and Hooker gave rise to the famous quip, reported by Walton, that *"The Forenoon Sermon spake* Canterbury, *and the Afternoon*, Geneva" (*Lives*, 200). Whitgift at last put an end to the dispute by silencing Travers and finally acceding to Hooker's request that he might have the quiet of some country place. So it was that Hooker went to Boscomb, near Salisbury, and eventually to Bishopsbourne in Kent, and in these places he composed his books of *Ecclesiastical Polity*, having laid their foundations during his time at the Temple. Hooker's life might be seen as a progress toward this great work, his early years preparing him for it, and his preaching at the Temple the turning point for his real life's work—and his death.

In the remainder of the *Life of Hooker*, Walton dwells principally on the composition and disposition of the *Ecclesiastical Polity*, offering first a vivid scene of their being read to Pope Clement VIII. The story, in Walton's lively prose, is the first in a set of dramatic scenes that enhance Hooker's reputation and fame. Having heard the first book of the *Polity*, the pope, Walton says, exclaimed, *"There is no Learning that this man hath not searcht into; nothing too hard for his understanding: this man indeed deserves the name of an Author; his Books will get reverence by Age, for there is in them such seeds of Eternity, that if the rest be like this, they shall last till the last fire shall consume all Learning"* (*Lives*, 212). Unlike Gauden, Walton does not try to analyze the contents of Hooker's work, except in rather large terms; he prefers to trace the fame and describe the reception, from Whitgift's approval to the commendation of Queen Elizabeth and her successors, James and Charles I. Hooker's humility and self-deprecation are indeed used to emphasize his role as the principal theological thinker of England, whose thought informs all of Europe. The quietness of his temper seems to emphasize the greatness of his achievement. And as if to answer obliquely the derogatory comments of Gauden on Hooker's dull preaching, Walton describes Hooker's pastoral ministry among the simple people of Bishopsbourne:

> His Sermons were neither long nor earnest, but uttered with a grave zeal, and an humble voice; his eyes always fixt on one place to prevent his imagination from wandring, insomuch, that he seem'd to study as he spake; the design of his Sermons (as indeed of all his Discourses) was to shew Reasons for what he spake; and with these Reasons, such a kind of Rhetorick, as did rather convince and perswade, than frighten men into piety; studying not so much for matter . . . as for apt illustrations to inform and teach his unlearned Hearers by familiar Applications; never labouring by hard words, and then by needless distinctions and sub-distinctions, to *amuse* his Hearers, and get glory to himself; but glory only to God. Which intention, he would often say, was as discernable in a Preacher, *as a Natural from an Artificial beauty.* (*Lives*, 218)

We have no examples of Hooker's preaching at this time, though fragments of earlier sermons survive that do show a directness and simplicity.[4] Yet one detects in Walton's panegyric his own preferences rather than a true account of what and how Hooker spoke.

In the final pages of his *Life*, Walton shows Hooker in his parsonage, anticipating the kind of dedicated, holy life that he will next describe in his *Life of Herbert*. We see Hooker in conversation with his friend Hadrian Saravia, who is introduced purposefully; for Saravia was one of the leading exponents of the episcopacy, seeing in it a divine institution. Walton writes that in Hooker's last year of life, 1600, he regularly saw Saravia, and told him *"That he did not beg a long life of God, for any other reason, but to live to finish his three remaining Books of POLITY"* (*Lives*, 223). But Walton adds in words that are richly ambiguous, "And God heard his prayers, though he denied the Church the benefit of them, as compleated by himself; and 'tis thought he hastened his own death, by hastening to give life to his Books."

In a substantial appendix to his *Life*, as well as in a long letter from George Cranmer to Hooker (of February 1598), Walton provides additional information about the fate of Hooker's *Ecclesiastical Polity*. Walton has wished us to think ill of Joan Hooker, who "staid not a comely time to bewail her Widdow-hood" (*Lives*, 230). But within a month of

Hooker's death, Whitgift "sent one of his Chaplains to enquire of [her], for the three remaining Books of Polity, writ by her Husband: of which she would not, or could not give any account." Later the archbishop brought her to Lambeth, where he questioned her closely, and she confessed to him *"That one Mr. Charke, and another Minister that dwelt near Canterbury, came to her, and desired that they might go into her Husbands Study, and look upon some of his Writings: and that there they two burnt and tore many of them, assuring her, that they were Writings not fit to be seen, & that she knew nothing more concerning them"* (*Lives*, 231). She was discovered the next morning dead in her Westminster lodgings, her new husband suspected and questioned for the death, but he was declared innocent.

This extraordinary, colorful, and highly circumstantial account was treated as the final word on Hooker's *Ecclesiastical Polity* until C. J. Sisson in the 1940s examined the court and chancery records of the case in the Public Record Office in London, discovered Walton's errors, and vindicated Mrs. Hooker.[5] More recent studies have shown that the last three books were very much Hooker's, just as Gauden believed and as he published them.[6] Yet so credible and convincing was Walton that his *Life of Hooker*, first published on its own in 1665, took the place of Gauden's "Life" in the 1666 folio of Hooker's *Works*, and it remained firmly attached to every subsequent edition of Hooker down to the present century.

The Life of Mr. George Herbert

Having written his *Life of Hooker*, which, with the general approval of the episcopacy, particularly of Sheldon, replaced the defective life by Gauden, Walton now turned confidently to his "labor of love," the *Life of George Herbert* (1593–1633), *"writ, chiefly to please my self: but, yet, not without some respect to posterity; for though he was not a man that the next age can forget; yet, many of his particular acts and vertues might have been neglected, or lost, if I had not collected and presented them to the Imitation of those that shall succeed us: for I humbly conceive writing to be both a safer and truer preserver of mens Vertuous actions, then tradition, especially as 'tis manag'd in this age"* (*Lives*, 6). Walton certainly could have been under no special obligation to write of Herbert, nor was he in any hurry to complete the *Life*, as he informs us in his general preface of 1675. The *Life* first appeared independently in 1670, and within a few months it was published again in the collected *Lives* (1675), that is, with Donne, Wotton, and Hooker. Although Walton is not likely to have known Herbert personally, he obviously appealed to Walton as a *"great example of holiness,"* one whom he had already portrayed as a notably pious man in his revised *Life of Donne* (1658).[7]

Near the end of this expanded version, Walton lists a number of Donne's "dear friends and benefactors," including Sir Henry Goodyer, Sir Robert Drury, Sir Henry Wotton, Henry King, and Lady Magdalen Herbert, George Herbert's mother, whose funeral sermon Walton had heard Donne preach in 1627. Of Herbert himself, Walton declares that he was a man "of primitive piety," the remarkable author of *The Temple*, "A Book, in which by declaring his own spiritual Conflicts, he hath Comforted and raised many a dejected and discomposed Soul, and charmed them into sweet and quiet thoughts: A Book, by the frequent reading whereof, and the assistance of that Spirit that seemed to inspire the Author, the Reader may attain habits of *Peace* and *Piety*, and all the gifts of the *Holy Ghost* and *Heaven:* and may by still reading, still keep those sacred fires burning upon the Altar of so pure a heart, as shall free it from the anxieties of this world, and keep it fixt upon things that are above" (*Lives*, 63–64). Moreover, Walton invokes the benevolent spirit of Herbert in all versions of *The Compleat Angler*, giving in full "Vertue," a poem by the "Holy Mr. *Herbert*" that illustrates the pleasantness of remembered meadows and fragrant flowers.[8] Walton suggests that "Sweet day, so cool, so calm, so bright" is mostly a poem of gentle nostalgia; but of course it is much more than this, for it most especially describes the life of the well-seasoned soul, "Like seasoned Timber" that never "gives," even at the end of time. Probably Walton had decided on the shape and direction of Herbert's life long before he came to write it, and the passing years fixed his views more firmly. The frequent reprinting of *The Temple* (first and second editions in 1633, then 1634, 1635, 1638, 1641, 1656, and so on[9]) and the appearance of *The Country Parson* in 1652 are testimony to Herbert's popularity, which Walton's *Life* celebrates, though his interest is principally to give a portrait of the ideal English pastor at work in an untroubled English church, rather than in the poetry (or prose) itself. Yet one may safely conclude that Walton's *Life of Herbert* affected the *literary* response to Herbert for generations of readers, who may have supposed as well that the Stuart church provided a culture that could sustain such a man as George Herbert. Walton is indeed a master of invention, and one of the ablest creators of an Edenic time, which, like other golden eras, never really existed.

Among Walton's principal reasons for writing the *Life of Herbert* was his desire to exalt the church and those persons, often well born and aristocratic, who serve it professionally. The priestly calling is a noble one, Walton is saying, and no less important than any other—indeed, rather higher in worth than other vocations, and certainly to be chosen over an academic life. Walton cultivated the friendship of many clergy, some very distinguished, and he himself was connected, as we have seen, through family relationships to Archbishop Cranmer and to Bishop Ken. Nowhere does Walton's love for these people and the church they share appear so generously as in his *Life of Herbert*.

The material Walton gathered for this *Life* came especially through Arthur Woodnoth, though Walton does not explicitly give him credit. How Walton became acquainted with Woodnoth is not clear, but the two men were both in trade at the same time, Walton as a draper in Fleet Street and Chancery Lane, Woodnoth as a goldsmith in Foster Lane. Woodnoth, a first cousin of Nicholas Ferrar, helped him to secure lands at Little Gidding in Huntingdonshire, where Ferrar and his extended family established themselves in about 1625. There the family lived a retired life devoted to prayer and good works. A chapel was constructed where members of the family worshiped, keeping most of the canonical hours and also a regular "night watch" in which the whole of the Psalter was recited.

Woodnoth must have become acquainted with Herbert some time in the late 1620s, for he was frequently at Little Gidding; Herbert was employing him to help in the rebuilding of Leighton Bromswold, a decayed parish only about seven miles distant, of which Herbert had been given the care in mid-1626, shortly after his taking orders. Woodnoth in 1633 attended the dying Herbert at Bemerton, near Salisbury, and took from him the manuscript of *The Temple*, which Woodnoth had conveyed to Nicholas Ferrar at Little Gidding. These rich details occur in Walton, who must have received them from Woodnoth at least 20 years before starting to write *The Life of Herbert*, for Woodnoth died in about 1651. Alongside his reminiscences of conversations with Woodnoth, Walton also had at hand Nicholas Ferrar's preface to *The Temple*, and most important, he read the account of Barnabas Oley (1602–1686), who had been associated with Little Gidding and who edited Herbert's *Remains* in 1652, which included his "Prefatory View of the Life."

But Walton's plan in his *Life of Herbert* is distinctively his own, with a selection and arrangement of details independent of his likely sources. He was enormously attracted to Herbert's *Country Parson*, already mentioned, a manual and guide designed particularly for rural priests but of interest to any who care for souls. This book displays a beauty of devotion and a deeply sacramental view of life; it offers a moving view of the ideal pastor while at the same time recommending that everyone should live "a godly, righteous, and sober life." Walton recognizes Herbert as the perfect embodiment of the ideal pastor of his own *Country Parson*. This is the man who expresses that life of devotion and prayer that Jeremy Taylor described in *Holy Living* (1650), a life that ends in an exemplary death, described also by Taylor in *Holy Dying* (1651). As we have seen, Walton typically writes of his subjects as living and preparing for death, and in his *Life of Herbert* he most notably develops this theme.

In his introduction to the *Life*, Walton joins Herbert with Donne and Wotton: "*And though Mr.* George Herbert . . . *were to me a stranger as to his person, for I have only seen him: yet since he was, and was worthy to be their friend, and very many of his have been mine; I judge it may not be unacceptable to those that knew any of them in their lives, or do now know them by mine, or their own Writings, to see this Conjunction of them after their deaths; without which, many things that concern'd them, and some things that concern'd the Age in which they liv'd, would be less perfect, and lost to posterity*" (*Lives*, 259). Thus Walton gives his reasons for writing of Herbert, to which we may add those many natural inclinations that led him to undertake this work; and he concludes with customary modesty that "if I have prevented [that is, preceded or stood in the way of] any abler person [in writing the biography], I beg pardon of him, and my Reader" (*Lives*, 259).

Walton carefully constructs the *Life of Herbert* to show Herbert's aristocratic background and academic brilliance on the one hand, and his pious devotion to the priesthood and to his congregations on the other. Walton also demonstrates Herbert's desire to please his mother, Magdalen, Lady Danvers, who is characterized as a person of piety and warmth, under whose holy guidance Herbert naturally thrives; he cannot be other than deferential to so grand and so good a mother. Herbert's happy submission to his mother's will is made parallel with his secular life and his court ambitions and his success as University Orator at Cambridge. But after the death of powerful friends and of King James himself (in 1625), Herbert retired to a private and solitary place in Kent, after which he determined to cast aside his old life for a new one and so to enter sacred orders "to which his dear Mother had often persuaded him" (*Lives*, 277). Not long after, Magdalen died; but in place of his nourishing mother, Herbert finds a second mother. When Herbert himself lies dying and is attended by Edmund Duncon, a friend from

Little Gidding, Duncon asks him how he should like to pray. *"What Prayers?* to which, Mr. *Herberts* answer was, *O Sir, the Prayers of my Mother, the Church of* England, *no other Prayers are equal to them!"* (*Lives*, 308). Clayton Lein has deftly pointed out the theme that Walton so convincingly weaves into the whole design of the *Life:* there is a structural pattern of two mothers that reinforces the "meaning of submission and humility within religious life, Herbert's earthly mother leading her son to the behavior most needful for his spiritual growth."[10]

Another important organizing feature of the *Life* encloses Herbert with "holy friendships." Magdalen Herbert (that is, Lady Danvers by her second marriage) is again the connecting and central figure, for Walton sensitively portrays her as astutely caring for all her children, winning the admiration of everyone. Of George, whose wit and innocence was apparent from childhood, a boy who "seem'd to be marked out for piety," the prudent mother "well knowing, that he might easily lose, or lessen that virtue and innocence which her advice and example had planted in his mind," provides for him a worthy tutor at Trinity College, Cambridge; the man is the eminent Dr. Neville, master of the college, who "knew the excellencies of his Mother, and how to value such a friendship" (*Lives*, 262–63).

With George at Cambridge lodged in his study, Walton shifts his narrative in order to tell yet more about this remarkable woman. When George was about four years old, her husband died; continuing about 12 years a widow, she then was married "happily to a Noble Gentleman, the Brother and Heir of the Lord *Danvers* Earl of *Danby*, who did highly value both her person and the most excellent endowments of her mind" (*Lives*, 263). But before her marriage to Danvers, she was anxious to settle her eldest son, Edward, at Oxford, and she moved there with him and some of her younger sons. Having provided Edward with a "fit" tutor, she continued in Oxford, "and still kept him in a moderate awe of her self: and so much under her own eye, as to see and converse with him daily; but she managed this power over him without any such rigid sourness, as might make her company a torment to her Child; but with such a sweetness and complyance with the recreations and pleasures of youth, as did incline him willingly to spend much of his time in the company of his dear and careful Mother: which was to her great content" (*Lives*, 264). Magdalen Herbert remained in Oxford four years, and there she gained the "acquaintance and friendship with most of any eminent worth or learning, that were at that time in or near that University," and most particularly with John Donne, who wrote, according to Walton, his elegy "The Autumnal" in her honor—Walton's testimony has no corroboration. Walton's purpose in mentioning Donne here is to give further evidence of Magdalen Herbert's strength of character and capacity for friendship, especially with one who would become well known to her son George Herbert.

In a way that becomes increasingly evident in Walton's *Lives*, time moves quickly, or it is warped and turns back on itself. Walton wants to make his purpose clear and to emphasize the great themes of his *Life*: to demonstrate the influence of Herbert's family, especially his mother, but also of ideal friendship. Walton says that he might offer "more demonstrations" of the friendship between Magdalen Herbert and Donne; but he is ready now to resume his account of Herbert, yet he wants to look forward briefly to that time in 1627 when Donne would preach the funeral sermon of his dear friend Magdalen, Lady Danvers. Walton recalls (and looks forward) to this time: "I saw and heard . . . *Donne* (who was then Dean of *St. Pauls*) weep, and preach her Funeral Sermon, in the Parish-Church of *Chelsey* near *London*, where she now rests in her quiet Grave: and where we must now leave her, and return to her Son *George*, whom we left in his Study in *Cambridge*" (*Lives,* 267).

Yet Herbert's mother remains a powerful figure throughout the *Life*, exemplifying care, virtue, piety—and of course friendship. Toward the end of the *Life*, Walton introduces Nicholas Ferrar, not to replace Magdalen Herbert so much as to provide another remarkable character, who occupies a similar position in Herbert's later years. Walton stops his narrative of Herbert in order to describe Ferrar's exemplary life, his genius for friendship, and his devotion to the English church—Walton calls him "eminent for his obedience to his Mother, *the Church of England*" (*Lives*, 309). The account of Ferrar's life and his establishing the community at Little Gidding, and the round of devotions over which he presided there, occupies a large place in the whole *Life of Herbert*, and it is situated near the end of Herbert's life in a way that balances the description of Magdalen Herbert near the beginning of his life. Herbert's actual relationship to Nicholas Ferrar was slight, for the two men were separated by a considerable distance; but the association of "Saint" Nicholas with George Herbert is significant, for it underlines unmistakably the direction toward which Herbert's life is leading. After bringing Ferrar through his "course of piety" to his death in 1637 (four years after the death of Herbert), Walton draws his moral: "Mr. *Farrers* [*sic*], and Mr. *Herberts* devout lives, were both so noted, that the general report of their sanctity gave them occasion to renew that slight acquaintance which was begun at their being Contemporaries in *Cambridge;* and this new holy friendship was long maintain'd without any interview, but only by loving and endearing Letters" (*Lives*, 312).

Walton thus manages to include in his *Life of Herbert* the lives also of two others—Magdalen Herbert and Nicholas Ferrar—while skillfully linking them to his emerging portrait of Herbert himself. Walton is a master of narrative within narrative, plotting seamlessly the character he wishes to reveal through highly selective details, pleasing anecdotes, and digressions that never seem out of place or irrelevant. The cheerful account of Herbert's marriage to Jane Danvers may remind us of Donne's "great mistake," or Hooker's unhappiness. These marriages all occur suddenly, yet Herbert's is the only one whose haste may be excused. Jane was the favorite of her father's nine daughters, and he had designed her to be Herbert's wife. Unfortunately, Danvers died before a meeting could be arranged:

> Yet some friends to both parties, procur'd their meeting; at which time a mutual affection entred into both their hearts, as a Conqueror enters into a surprized City, and Love having got such possession govern'd, and made there such Laws and Resolutions, as neither party was able to resist; insomuch, that she chang'd her name into *Herbert*, the third day after this first interview.... This haste might in others be thought a *Love-phrensie*, or worse: but it was not; for they had wooed so like Princes, as to have select Proxies: such, as were true friends to both parties; such as well understood Mr. *Herberts*, and her temper of mind; and also their Estates so well, before this Interview, that, the suddenness was justifiable, by the strictest Rules of prudence: And the more, because it prov'd so happy to both parties; for the eternal lover of Mankind, made them happy in each others mutual and equal affections, and compliance. (*Lives*, 286)

Walton's account of this courtship is highly improbable, for Sir John Danvers, Jane's cousin, had been Herbert's stepfather for 20 years. It would be strange indeed if Herbert had laid eyes on her for the first time only three days before he married her.[11] Yet their love, joy, and content received "a daily augmentation . . . as was only improvable in Heaven" (287). Unlike the shrewish Mrs. Hooker, who forced her husband to "rock the cradle," Jane promoted George Herbert's ministry in his poor country parish of Bemerton, helping him, in one notable anecdote, to support a poor old woman with the practical gift of a pair of blankets and the message *"That she would see and be acquainted with her, when her house was built at* Bemerton" (*Lives*, 292).

Walton hovers affectionately over Herbert's brief ministry of only three years, remarking, for example, on the kind of sermons Herbert preached—all of them, we are led to understand, sensible, correct, helpful, and strictly related to the feasts and fasts of the church. He was conscientious, dutiful but also inspiring, so that when he rang his bell for prayers during the day, "some of the meaner sort of his Parish, [who] did so love and reverence Mr. *Herbert*, that they would let their Plow rest . . . that they might also offer their devotions to God with him: and would then return back to their Plow" (*Lives*, 302). His favorite recreation was music, about which Walton offers a few reflections; but he has little to say about the poetry, and one may suppose that Walton discovered only the poems' frequently smooth surface and little of the conflict and sorrow that lie within so many of them. Walton lets Herbert fulfill his literary ambitions by having him discount them in the well-known words to Duncon during his last sickness: "*Sir, I pray deliver this little Book to my dear brother* Farrer, *and tell him he shall find in it a picture of the many spiritual Conflicts that have past betwixt God and my Soul, before I could subject mine to the will of* Jesus my Master: *in whose service I have now found perfect freedom; desire him to read it: and then, if he can think it may turn to the advantage of any dejected poor Soul, let it be made publick: if not, let him burn it: for I and it, are less than the least of God's mercies*" (314). The concluding pages of the *Life* are affectionately drawn; Walton lingers over Herbert's death, not quite letting him go: "Thus he liv'd, and thus he dy'd like a Saint, unspotted of the World, full of Alms-deeds, full of Humility, and all the examples of a vertuous life" (319). No other of Walton's *Lives* portrays such a perfect ending, for no other depicts a life so flawless from the beginning.

The Life of Dr. Sanderson, Late Bishop of Lincoln

Robert Sanderson (1587–1663) may be the least familiar to us of Walton's heroes, but he was eminent in his own day as a staunch royalist and was revered as the author of influential works on casuistry, or "cases of conscience," some of which appeared with the *Life* in 1678. Sanderson, who was noted for his unyielding support of the episcopacy, was to become the Restoration bishop of Lincoln; he was admired also both for his pastoral and his intellectual gifts. Although Walton must have wished to write of such a bishop to provide an appropriate complement to his life of Herbert, the pious yet learned country parson, one may still wonder why Walton selected Sanderson. There were other remarkable men, as David Novarr notes: Brian Duppa, William Juxon, John Bramhall, John Earle, Jeremy Taylor, and Henry King, a list that easily might be expanded to include such reliable figures as John Cosin, the learned bishop of Durham; any one of these men seems as worthy of a life study as Sanderson. But Walton was moved to write of Sanderson because of Bishop Morley's encouragement and probable advice (Novarr, 367).

Morley, we remember, was Walton's old friend, now of nearly 50 years, under whose roof Walton had been living for a very long time. Walton admired him enormously and would likely have written Morley's life if that were possible: but one could not write of the living, and so Walton wrote instead of Morley's great friend. The two had known each other at Oxford and at Great Tew, that remarkable "little college" presided over by Lucius Cary and attended by the "ever memorable" John Hales, William Chillingworth, Henry Hammond, and others similarly minded. They had together attended King Charles during his imprisonment on the Isle of Wight in 1648; they had together suffered the sequestration of their livings but lived to recover them in the Restoration. Walton thus determined to express Morley's love for Sanderson as a kind of devoted offering from him to Morley, whose spirit certainly directs the general movement of the *Life*. But Walton responded to his task in a way that only Walton himself could do.

Having written of the ideal country priest from a layman's point of view, Walton saw a new opportunity to describe an ideal bishop. In both the *Life of Herbert* and the *Life of Sanderson*, Walton wishes to describe the particular beauty, as he sees it, of the English church, and the ugliness of nonconformity and division. Novarr cogently discerns this purpose. Walton sought "to present such a picture of a son and father of the Church as would win from the general reader sympathy and support for the High Church and the Episcopal position. He would rectify the stereotype of the dogmatic diocesan, remote in demean and resplendent in luxury, would set in its place the long-suffering, temperate, mild, and humble overseer of the realm of God. Conversely, he would reveal the dissenter of tender conscience to be a temporizing zealot, an unscrupulous schismatic governed only by self-interest" (Novarr, 397). The *Life of Sanderson* thus provided Walton with a means for extolling episcopacy and the Restoration church. For him, Sanderson provides an episcopal continuation of the properly Reformed church that Hooker defined, Donne celebrated, Wotton acclaimed, and Herbert modeled. One may easily see how closely linked are all of Walton's *Lives* by their common intellectual and theological outlook. The *Life of Sanderson*, however, is unusual in its outspoken, even audacious declaration of intent.

When he wrote this *Life*, Walton was in his mid-80s; he had lived through the years leading up to the Civil Wars, and he had seen the misery and disruption of those wars; he had chafed under the Cromwell interregnum, and joyed in the Restoration of the monarchy—and he would live almost to the end of the second Charles's reign. Walton has reached an extremely confident stage in this, his last principal work; although age has not changed his views, it has provided him with the powerful determination to speak them forthrightly. His unassailable belief in the "good old way" was never so strong,[12] and he was inclined to draw a sharp difference between heroes and villains. For him Sanderson is a hero, who stands helpfully in the place of Morley, about whom he would have wished to write; nonconformists of all colors are discarded and treated as ignominious traitors. We may suppose that Walton, like Morley, would have been distressed by Charles II's vacillation and expedient support of the High Church party.[13]

Walton begins the *Life of Sanderson* in his typically apologetic manner, but this time his diffidence seems very much a rhetorical gesture. Walton knows that he must (and will) present a fit picture of Sanderson and an appropriate preface to his work, although Sanderson desired in his will that none of his writings should be printed:

> And, though my Age might have procur'd me a Writ of Ease, and that secur'd me from all further trouble in this kind; yet I met with such perswasions to begin, and so many willing Informers since . . . that when I found my self faint, and weary of the burthen with which I had loaden my self, and ready to lay it down; yet time and new strength hath at last brought it to be what it now is, and presented to the Reader, and with it this desire; That he will take notice, that Dr. *Sanderson* did in his Will or last Sickness advertise, that after his death nothing of his might be printed; because *that might be said to be his, which indeed was not;* and also for that *he might have chang'd his opinion since he first writ it*. And though these Reasons ought to be regarded, yet regarded so, as he resolves in that Case of Conscience concerning *rash Vows*, that there may appear very good second Reasons, why we may forbear to perform them. (*Lives*, 345–46)

Sanderson himself seems implicitly to give permission that his works should be published; yet "they ought to be read as we do *Apocriphal Scripture;* to explain, but not oblige us to so firm a belief of what is here presented as his" (*Lives*, 346). Walton intends to show that Sanderson is learned and pious in whatever ways are available to him.

The *Life of Sanderson* is loosely yet carefully organized. It is much more a "life and times" study than any of the previous *Lives*, and it is much more obviously moralistic and sententious. Sanderson's life is connected to the political and ecclesiastical world in which he lived—at least as Walton observed it. His piety and virtue is clear from the beginning, only increasing with age, and so he becomes worthy of the bishopric to which he is finally preferred. Sanderson is not seen to move from a secular to a clerical and holier life in a dramatic way, as is Donne or Herbert, or even Wotton. His development is rather more like that of Hooker, whose inclination for learning and piety becomes more profound over time. Like Hooker, Sanderson too must face opposition, principally from the ignorant and unperceptive. Yet as with the other *Lives*, Walton manages to portray a remarkably sympathetic character who displays virtues without being overwhelmed by them.

Sanderson might come close to being flat and featureless, but the piety and virtue to which he is dedicated is accompanied by "a sorrow for the infirmities of his being too timorous and bashful" (*Lives*, 354). Any deficiency is turned to good use, however; for during the term of his proctorship at Oxford, Walton shows him to be a person whose modesty is perceived as severity. Even Gilbert Sheldon, a younger contemporary who would one day be archbishop of Canterbury, was, on his going to the university, commended to Sanderson's attention by his godfather, Sanderson's own father. Sanderson in due course invites Sheldon to his rooms: "But it seems Mr. *Sheldon* having (like a young man as he was) run into some such irregularity as made him conscious he had transgress'd his Statutes, did therefore apprehend the Proctor's invitation as an introduction of punishment; the fear of which made his Bed restless that night; but at their meeting the next morning, that fear vanished immediately by the Proctor's chearful countenance, and the freedom of the discourse of Friends" (*Lives*, 361). Walton cleverly shows the vigor yet also the meekness of Sanderson's character while indicating the inception of an important personal (and eventually ecclesiastical and episcopal) friendship. Sanderson's diffidence is illustrated again on a different occasion by his effort to preach without a script. Accompanied by his friend Henry Hammond, Sanderson is urged to forego his written sermon:

> At Dr. *Sanderson*'s going into the Pulpit, he gave his Sermon . . . into the hand of Dr. *Hammond*, intending to preach it as 'twas writ; but before he

had preach'd a third part, Dr. *Hammond* (looking on his Sermon as written) observed him to be out, and so lost as to the matter, that he also became afraid for him; for 'twas discernable to many of the plain Auditory: But when he had ended this short Sermon, as they two walk'd homeward, Dr. *Sanderson* said with much earnestness, *Good Doctor give me my Sermon, and know, that neither you, nor any man living, shall ever perswade me to preach again without my Books.* To which the reply was, *Good Doctor be not angry; for if I ever perswade you to preach again without Book, I will give you leave to burn all those that I am Master of.* (385)

Weakness is strength in Walton's description, for he is able to render his portrait of Sanderson more intimate and truthful. In his highly selective fashion, Walton invests certain incidents with implied revelation, association, and character.

When Sanderson leaves Oxford in 1618, he is presented to the rectory of Wibberton, near Boston, Lincolnshire, and then (the climate being unfavorable for his health) he goes to Boothby Pagnell (or, in Walton's phonetic spelling, "Boothby Pannel"), also in Lincolnshire, in the following year, where he was to remain, apart from another period at Oxford and the time also of his sequestration, until the Restoration. Walton provides a glimpse of Sanderson's life as a parish priest, reminiscent in his devotion and steadiness of George Herbert at Bemerton. Here he remained "in an obscure and quiet privacy, doing good daily both by word and by deed, as often as any occasion offer'd it self" (*Lives*, 367); but such "contented obscurity" is gently touched by his decision to wed "a complying and a prudent Wife" about whom Walton mentions almost nothing else, save that she was called Anne and was the daughter of Henry Nelson, rector of Haugham, "a man of noted worth and learning" (*Lives*, 368, 363–64). Anne was as worthy a helpmate, it would seem, as Jane Herbert. Walton evidently has strong views, though quite usual for his time, about domestic happiness and the role of women in providing the comfort and help necessary for their husbands.

Now in the midst of his narrative, Walton describes the feverish times, from the Long Parliament, summoned in 1640, to the death of Laud in 1645, to Sanderson's own ejection from his living at Boothby Pagnell, to his forced retirement to London or else to places about which Walton is extremely vague. But there is no imprecision in his account of the dark forces that were surrounding good men like Sanderson, nor in Sanderson's boldness in meeting these enemies of truth and reason:

In this time of his retirement, when the common people were amaz'd & grown giddy by the many falshoods and misapplications of Truths frequently vented in Sermons; when they wrested the Scripture by challenging God to be of their party, and call'd upon him in their prayers to patronize their Sacriledge & zealous Frenzies, in this time he did so compassionate the generality of this misled Nation, that though the times threatned danger, yet he then hazarded his safety by writing the large and bold Preface now extant before his last 20 Sermons. (*Lives*, 392)

This publication appeared in 1655, about the same time as the chance meeting of Walton with Sanderson in London, at a bookseller's. He is wearing "sad-coloured clothes . . . far from being costly," and Walton tells of their conversation with his sure touch for realistic detail, the kind of stroke that makes his life writing so memorable:

The place of our meeting was near to *little Britain*, where he had been to buy a Book, which he then had in his hand: we had no inclination to part presently; and therefore turn'd to stand in a corner under a Penthouse (for it began to rain) and immediately the wind rose, and the rain increased so much, that both became so inconvenient, as to force us into a cleanly house, where we had *Bread, Cheese, Ale,* & a *Fire* for our money. This rain and wind were so obliging to me, as to force our stay there for at least an hour, to my great content and advantage; for in that time he made to me many useful observations with much clearness and conscientious freedom. (393)

What Walton remembers of this pleasant conversation relates principally to the reforms of the Parliament that had abolished the familiar liturgy of the Book of Common Prayer "to the scandal of so many devout and learned men." Sanderson, according to Walton, commends the old forms of worship that now have been replaced by "needless debates about *Free-will, Election*, and *Reprobation*, of which, and many like Questions, we may be safely ignorant, because Almighty God intends not to lead us to Heaven by hard Questions, but by meekness and charity, and a frequent practice of Devotion" (394). These sentiments express Walton's views precisely, whether or not they reflect exactly what was said on this occasion.

By his introduction of this "conversation out of the rain," Walton skillfully characterizes his subject, his times, and his own strong views. He is careful here, as always, to avoid mere summary or abstract argument while advancing a general belief. Sanderson remains "quiet and harmless," yet determined to keep the faith against all opponents—though Walton leaves the theological terms of debate vague, even suggesting that they are irrelevant. Peaceableness, indeed, needs no theology; Walton condemns those who have upset the nation and its historic religion: "All corners of the Nation were fill'd with Covenanters, Confusion, Committee-men and Soldiers, serving each other to their several ends, of revenge, or power, or profit; and these Committee-men and Soldiers were most of them so possest with this Covenant, that they became like those that were infected with that dreadful Plague of *Athens;* the Plague of which Plague was, that they by it became maliciously restless to get into company, and to joy . . . when they had infected others" (*Lives*, 382). The gentle, irenic, "honest Izaak" has no shortage of terms for describing these enemies of church and state: the Reformers are called "scruple-mongers," "covetous," "cross-grained," filled with the stupidity and venom of "malice and madness," scarce credible.

This time, more than 20 years past when Walton writes, is vividly recalled. But the Restoration would spell an end to the troubles. Walton links his happiness in remembering the time with the hero of his biography, as an especially poignant and notable passage demonstrates:

> Toward the end of . . . 1659, when the many mixt Sects, and their Creators and merciless Protestors, had led or driven each other into a Whirlpool of Confusion: when amazement and fear had seiz'd them, and their accusing Consciences gave them an inward and fearful intelligence, that the God which they had long serv'd, was now ready to pay them such wages as he does always reward *Witches* with for their obeying him: When these wretches were come to foresee an end of their cruel reign, by our King's return; and such Sufferers as Dr. *Sanderson* (and with him many of the oppressed Clergy and others) could foresee the cloud of their afflictions would be dispers'd by it: Then, in the beginning of the year following, the King was by God restored to us, and we to our known Laws and Liberties; and a general joy and peace seem'd to breath through the 3 Nations. Then were the suffering Clergy freed from their Sequestration, restor'd to their Revenues, and to a liberty to adore, praise, and pray to God in such order as their Consciences and Oaths had formerly obliged them. . . . Dr. *Sanderson* and his dejected Family rejoyc'd to see this day, and be of this number. (*Lives*, 400)

The time is now ready to recognize the wisdom of Sanderson. The king, Walton says, entrusted Sheldon "to commend to him fit men to supply the then vacant Bishopricks," and none is fitter than Sanderson, who is given the see of Lincoln, in which office he is consecrated at the end of October 1660.

Walton's *Life of Sanderson* reaches its climax at this point, for the years of revolution and war have come to an end in the revival and continuity of the monarchy and the episcopacy. Sanderson has been living all of this time so that he can act according to the providential fulfillment of the nation and the church. His life of devotion, consistent prayer, and deep learning is now at the service of the restored episcopacy—in which Walton's great friend Morley is also a principal actor, though necessarily a mute figure in the present story. Sanderson lived hardly three years in his new dignity (Herbert's pastoral life was equally brief), but he provided important leadership at the Savoy Conference, called in 1661 for dealing with the concerns of the nonconformists, and he helped with liturgical renewal; the famous preface to the Book of Common Prayer (1661) is, according to Walton, Sanderson's composition (*Lives*, 405).[14]

Sanderson died as he lived—a holy life prepared him for a holy death. Walton closes this *Life*, as he has ended all of his *Lives*, with a detailed and expansive description of the sickbed. He shows Sanderson's ailing and declining days and hours, his repetition of Psalms and prayers, and his lifelong pattern of turning his first waking thoughts to God. His heart is fixed at last wholly on death, for which he longs and is well prepared. Walton's last words about Sanderson lead at last into what could have been his own epitaph. Sanderson's desire to die "seem'd to come from Heaven,"

> so [this desire] left him not, till his Soul ascended to that Region of blessed Spirits, whose Imployments are to joyn in consort with him, and sing *praise* and *glory* to that God, who hath brought them to that place, *into which sin and sorrow cannot enter.*
>
> Thus this pattern of *meekness* and primitive *innocence* chang'd this for a better life. 'Tis now too late to wish that my life may be like his; for I am in the eighty fifth year of my Age; but I humbly beseech Almighty God, that my death may; and do as earnestly beg of every Reader to say Amen.
>
> *Blessed is the man in whose Spirit there is no guile.* Psal. 32.2. (*Lives*, 414–15)

Thus the *Life of Sanderson* ends, the last and in some ways most successful of the *Lives*, for it is clearly integrated with the process of historical events and their development. This *Life* also manages chronology efficiently, uses records and documents authoritatively, and generally avoids digressions.

Yet Novarr is correct in suggesting that the *Life of Sanderson* is deficient in two respects: Walton champions Sanderson for his wisdom and his intellectual stature, yet he does not tell us what Sanderson wrote, apart from mechanically providing a few titles. Moreover, Walton is so partisan that he seems to cast all nonconformists in the same dark light but reveals Anglican divines of the Interregnum as moderate, long-suffering, and faithful apostles of truth. In the Restoration, Sanderson, a moderate High Churchman, appears to stand for the whole episcopacy, as if there were no variation of views. Walton's inclination had always been toward commentary and judgment, and in his *Sanderson* he is willing to reveal his hand and to speak in his own person. Perhaps these are not deficiencies so much as limitations that we have come to expect in Walton; they are simply more obvious in this last work. Walton never says very much about the creative work or writing of his subjects, whether to describe or to evaluate it. Nor has he ever felt warmly toward dissenters or revolutionaries of any stripe. Walton is deeply conservative and cautious from his early years, and he becomes more decided in his social and cultural outlook as he grows older.

Walton's revision of his *Life of Sanderson*, which appeared in 1681, not surprisingly shows little change, with only minor alterations. He has nothing new to add to the *Life*, and he has, in any case, a firmly fixed mind. Walton's decided sentiments are corroborated in another late work, the anonymously published *Love and Truth: in Two modest and peaceable Letters. Concerning The distempers of the present Times* (1680).[15] According to the title page, these letters are both "written from a quiet and Conformable *Citizen* of London, to two busie and Factious *Shop-keepers* in Coventry," the first one supposedly written in 1667, the second in 1679. The style is unmistakably Walton's, and the attitudes essentially the same as those he expresses in the *Life of Sanderson*. In these letters— really brief treatises—Walton again makes explicit the lesson of the *Life;* but in *Love and Truth*, Walton speaks directly without the imposition of a biographical study. He ends the first letter with the motto of *The Compleat Angler*, "Study to be quiet, and to do your own business" (1 Thessalonians 4:11), and repeats it again in the second letter. The latter is a particularly dark portrayal of the evils of nonconformity and the dreadfulness of rebellion, which is "like the *sin* of *Witchcraft*," a near relative of schism: "When the fire of *Schism* and *Rebellion* is kindled, no man knows where it will end."[16] Walton is furious as he remembers the Long Parliament, the evil John Lilburne, Hugh Peters, and "Cromwell the Tyrant," but he is generous in his belief that the Anglican way is filled with integrity and gentleness. In recalling the hideous despots of years past, Walton urges the recipient of his "letter" to compare them with "the holy life and happy death of Mr. *George Herbert*," which he disingenuously declares to be "plainly and I hope truly writ by Mr. *Isaac Walton*." In this *Life* one may find "a perfect pattern for an humble and devout Christian to imitate . . . And he that considers the restless lives, and uncomfortable deaths of [Lilburne and Peters], (who always liv'd like the *Salamander* in the fire of contention) and considers the dismal consequences of *Schism* and *Sedition*, will (if prejudice, or a malicious Zeal have not so blinded him, that he cannot see reason) be so convinc'd as to beg of God to give him a meek and quiet spirit, and that he may by his grace be prevented from being a busie body in what concerns him not" (*Love and Truth*, 37–38). "Honest Izaak" is not always gentle, nor is he particularly tolerant or forgiving. He is as passionate and decided in his views as are his opponents in theirs.[17]

Chapter Four

"A Re-creation of a Recreation":
The Compleat Angler

General Background

Walton is most familiarly known as the author of *The Compleat Angler*, a book that rivals Bunyan's *Pilgrim's Progress* and the Bible in popularity if number of editions, reprints, and translations indicates renown. Walton himself revised his best-known work extensively during his own lifetime—the first edition of 1653 is much more spare than the last and expanded sixth edition of 1676. The book seems never to have wanted readers, or at least editions, for more than 400 versions have followed since Walton's death, and the book, or at least its reputation, is still well regarded in our own time. Walton is also the eponymous hero of the early ecological movement, and many persons who could hardly begin to identify him have rejoiced in their association with the "Izaak Walton League" for saving natural habitats.

But *The Compleat Angler* was not as highly regarded in its own time as were the *Lives*, and Walton, along with his immediate contemporaries, may have seen it as a kind of corroboration of his *Donne* and *Wotton*. All of these works have much in common, for Walton must have intended them to reflect and comment on his stormy world; their common attitude and style certainly suggest closely linked composition, the three parts of a triptych, even though the *Angler* has a form quite different from the two *Lives*.

Walton's identification with the royalist cause is well known and implicit in all of his works, his wide friendships with many leading churchmen and bishops encouraging this enduring sympathy. Yet Walton's spirit tries to be irenic; he is usually content to speak to his times through the indirection of a fishing manual in which the countryside glows peacefully in spring weather, in which friends and innkeepers discourse happily on equal terms, in which the rivers are filled with trout, perch, and carp waiting to be caught and eager to be eaten. Walton's rusticity is reminiscent of Ben Jonson's poem "To Penshurst," in which

society and country are well organized and radiant—or of other similar
evocations, such as Thomas Carew's "To Saxham"[1] or Robert Herrick's
delightful scenes in his *Hesperides* (1648), a work almost exactly contemporary with *The Compleat Angler*.

The year in which Walton's book appeared marked a low point in the
lives of those loyal to the old regime: Charles I was dead, the court in
exile, the Anglican clergy dispersed, their livings sequestered, the Prayer
Book banished. What more could be destroyed? Even the Long Parliament, which provided continuity, however egregious, with the years
before the Civil Wars, was gone. The mood of dispossession occurs regularly in the writing of the defeated party, and Richard Lovelace, a
notable Cavalier who died in about 1655, was one of the most eloquent
of them. In a number of poems, he captures this sense of defeat, nostalgia, and confident defiance. In "The Grass-hopper," addressed to Walton's friend Charles Cotton, Lovelace allegorizes political and social ruin
by the "Poore verdant foole! . . . now green Ice!" The grasshopper must
succumb to the harsh weather and its own improvidence; but we—Cotton and Lovelace (and those of our mind)— "will create / A Genuine
Summer in each others breast,"

> And spite of this Cold Time and frosen Fate
>   Thaw us a warme seate to our rest.
> Our sacred harthes shall burne eternally
>   As Vestall Flames, the North-Wind, he
> Shall strike his frost-stretch'd Winges, dissolve and flye
>   This *Ætna* in Epitome.

Ever stubbornly defiant, Lovelace closes this poem, written shortly after
the death of Charles, by invoking confidence in the perpetual value of
friendship and the steady peace of an honest heart:

> Thus richer then untempted Kings are we,
>   That asking nothing, nothing need:
> Though Lord of all what Seas imbrace; yet he
>   That wants himselfe, is poore indeed.[2]

Such sentiments were commonly expressed during these early years of
the Interregnum, and they must have echoed Walton's own beliefs.

Mid-seventeenth-century English writing can, indeed, be characterized by its response to the Civil Wars and their aftermath and by the ways in which persons of Walton's disposition frequently confronted the world by turning away from it and finding quiet in stoic endurance, retirement, and contemplation. Andrew Marvell followed the Lord General Fairfax to his estate at Appleton House, in Yorkshire, and there wrote his greatest poems about harmony and "decent Order tame." The darkened world is "a rude heap together hurl'd," not as it once was or was imagined to be, "that happy Garden-state" in which the mind might enjoy the happiness of its own contemplation. The Anglican royalist Henry Vaughan retired to Wales, and as the "Silurist" wrote of "deep, but dazling darkness" (*Silex Scintillans*, 1650). Jeremy Taylor, removed from any hope of preferment in the banished church, wrote his *Holy Living* (1650) and *Holy Dying* (1651) from the Carbery estate in Carmarthenshire, counseling his patron on the principles of right action and a just conscience, prefacing his study with an account of "Religion painted upon Banners, and thrust out of Churches."[3]

In such times, Walton also turned fondly to a more graceful, imagined world of good sense and order: we must not forget that the subtitle of his book is "The contemplative man's recreation," and it is clear that he is pursuing those ideals shared by many of his literary and ecclesiastical friends. Walton's book is, of course, about catching fish: "*Angling* is an *Art*," he reminds us in his dedicatory remarks, and in his discourse "To the Reader," he enlarges on his purpose: "I undertake to acquaint the Reader with many things that are not usually known to every Angler; and I shall leave gleanings and observations enough to be made out of the experience of all that love and practise this recreation, to which I shall encourage them. For *Angling* may be said to be so like the *Mathematicks*, that it can ne'r be fully learnt; at least not so fully, but that there will still be more new experiments left for the tryal of other men that succeed us."[4] Yet *The Compleat Angler* was from the first more than a manual about fishing, in the way that Robert Burton's *Anatomy of Melancholy* (1621, 1652) expands its alleged subject into a miscellany of information and satire or that Sir Thomas Browne's *Urne-Buriall* and *Garden of Cyrus* (1658) explore the issues of death and immortality.

Sources

Walton's book seems not to extend much beyond its central subject, at least not as obviously as the books by Burton or Browne do; nevertheless, Walton includes far more than his topic demands: poems, songs (even the musical notation for one), recipes, reflections on the weather and on the general social climate. We recognize of course that the central subject of the book is angling, but the social and political circumstances that lie behind the book and surround its publication point to a significance much wider than that of mere "fish and fishing." Walton's book is "not unworthy the perusal of most Anglers," as the original title page declares, nor is it inappropriate for the recreative study of ruined clergy and royalists, the dispersed friends of the author—Anglicans, whether "anglers" or not. Walton is providing a general book of wisdom for hard times in the shape of a fishing manual.

The borrowings and adaptations are numerous, frequently explicit. In expanding *The Compleat Angler* from its relatively spare first edition to the later, longer, and more elaborate editions (culminating in the fifth edition of 1676), Walton unloads his commonplace book to produce a carefully wrought—though seemingly digressive—anthology of facts and opinions. Walton freely makes use of the angling and related literature that precedes him, especially Jan Dubravius, *De Piscinis et Piscium . . . naturis* (1547, trans. 1599), on the manufacture and maintenance of fish ponds; William Samuel, *Arte of Angling* (1577); Leonard Mascall, *A Booke of Fishing with Hooke and Line* (1590); Gervase Markham, *Cheape and Good Husbandry* (1614), which is based on earlier works; George Hakewill, *Apologie of the Power and Providence of God* (1627), on the fish-eating customs of the Romans; the list might be considerably lengthened.[5] Walton is fascinated by natural history, particularly when prodigious and strange. He refers to Pliny's *Natural History*, which he knew in Philemon Holland's translation of 1634, and he knew William Camden's *Chorographica descriptio* (translated also by Holland, 1610, 1637); Walton used these and other encyclopedic works, whether of geography, fish, or other creatures: Conrad Gesner, *Historia animalium* (1558, 1604, 1620), whose book 4 illustrates and describes every known species of salt- and freshwater fish; Edward Topsel, *Historie of Four-footed Beastes* (1607) and *Historie of Serpents* (1608); Sir Francis Bacon, *Sylva Sylvarum: or A Natural History* (1627). Walton also quotes from or refers to Christopher Marlowe, Michael Drayton, George Herbert, and John Donne, among a number of contemporary (or nearly contemporary) literary figures.

Although *The Compleat Angler* appeared in the most tempestuous of times, the book depicts a serene and peaceful world. Yet in spite of his seeming avoidance of tribulation, Walton in fact is commenting on his age, even offering useful instruction to any who will hear him. Far from being escapist, Walton is deeply involved in the suffering and concerns that were surrounding him. That he should choose to write a piscatory manual of some practical use might to us seem a strange way to reflect on urgent and continuing crises. Walton, however, is calling upon a literary tradition that begins with such classical authors as Hesiod and Vergil. It is doubtful whether he deliberately set out to imitate such predecessors, but he must have been aware of the forms deriving from these classical writers, for such forms—or genres—were commonly practiced in the late Renaissance. Such a friend as Michael Drayton would surely have made him aware, for example, of Vergil's *Georgics*. Although he was no scholar and had studied only rudimentary Latin, Walton would certainly have read something of Vergil and, like his better-educated friend, realized that Vergil was the supreme master of the bucolic myth, who celebrated rural life, praised peace, and hated war and revolution. Walton, we may suppose, was well introduced to these essential features of the georgic convention, with its emphasis on the superior moral qualities of the simple man, the one who tills the land and keeps gardens, whose pursuits are much worthier than those of the worldly urban man of affairs. The values that Walton expresses in *The Compleat Angler* are those of this simple man who lives quietly in modest dignity.[6]

The georgic tradition to which Walton is indebted implies necessarily a didactic strain. Walton is writing instructively, not only to teach the rudiments of successful angling (and the cultivation of fish habitats and the propagation of fish) but also to demonstrate how all persons may live peacefully in the natural world. Henry Reynolds, like Drayton another of Walton's literary friends, wrote pointedly in *Mythomystes* (subtitled "A short survay . . . of the nature and value of true poesy and depth of the ancients above our modern poets") of the importance of interpreting the moral significance of "nature." He urges the superiority of the classical writers over modern ones, principally because of their desire to instruct while also being elegant and felicitous. In his criticism of "modern" poets, Reynolds shows that he clearly understands the serious burden resting on all writers:

> Wee liue in a myste, blind and benighted; and since our first fathers disobedience poysoned himselfe and his posterity, Man is become the imperfectest and most deficient Animall of all the field; for then he lost that Instinct that the Beast retaines; though with him the beast, and with it the whole vegetable and generall Terrene nature also suffered, and still

groanes vnder the losse of their first purity, occasioned by his fall. What
concernes him now so neerely as to attend to the cultiuating or refining,
& thereby aduancing of his rationall part, to the purchase & regaining of
his first lost felicity?[7]

Reynolds's partial solution to the meanness of the times is for all writers
to "search for the knowledge of the wise and hidden wayes & workings
of our great Gods hand-maid, Nature" (Reynolds, 165). Reynolds is
describing the general wisdom to which Walton was responding, that is,
the moral utility of literary composition, with the implicit message that
external nature contains religious meaning, which ought to be displayed
in a fashion both pleasing and seductive.

One may appreciate how easily another popular literary form could
be merged with or grafted on to the georgic mode. *The Compleat Angler*
is indebted also to the pastoral tradition, of which Vergil's *Eclogues* are
the obvious classical model. But Walton is writing in the immediate
company that broadly includes Spenser's *Shepheardes Calendar* (1579),
The Faerie Queene, notably book 6 (1596), and Milton's *Lycidas* (1637).
The essential requirement of pastoral writing is the contrast (implied or
asserted) between city and country to the obvious advantage of the latter, where the landscape is conventionally and perpetually arcadian,
inhabited by happy persons. Phineas Fletcher, whom Walton commends
as "an excellent Divine, and an excellent Angler" (*Angler*, 334), provided one particularly auspicious example of the pastoral eclogue, for he
turns his rural characters into fishermen in his seven *Piscatorie Eclogs*
(1633).[8]

"The Anglican Way"

Although Walton certainly celebrates the country—where else can
angling better occur?—his rustic world is decidedly conventionalized,
and his evocations of the chaste outdoors owe more to the imagination
than to seventeenth-century England. Walton casts his book in the form
of a dialogue covering several days' walk, each day ending with "a good
dish of meat" (*Angler*, 216), the reward of a successful catch. Walton,
who takes the role of "Piscator" (the fisherman), leads his willing student through the fine points of effective angling. Piscator advises his
"scholar," called "Venator" (a onetime hunter, now converted to the better life of fishing), that the day will draw to a comfortable close: "I'le
now lead you to an honest Ale-house where we shall find a cleanly room,

Lavender in the Windows, and twenty *Ballads* stuck about the wall; there my Hostess (which I may tell you, is both cleanly and handsome and civil) hath drest many a one for me [in this case a chub], and shall now dress it after my fashion, and I warrant it good meat" (216). Venator is agreeably hungry, so it is good that he and Piscator arrive promptly at the "cleanly" inn: "Come Hostess, how do you? Will you first give us a cup of your best drink, and then dress this *Chub*, as you drest my last . . . ? but you must do me one courtesie, it must be done instantly."

On another day, the companions are fishing for trout, and Piscator lands a "gallant" one. What shall we do with him? Venator asks. "Marry e'en eat him to supper," comes the reply and the thought again of ending the day at a house where the linen is white and smells of lavender. But for the present, they will rest near a honeysuckle hedge during a gentle rain shower that falls "so gently upon the teeming earth, and gives yet a sweeter smell to the lovely flowers that adorn these verdant Meadows" (*Angler*, 231). Piscator reflects upon the landscape in one of the fullest pastoral sections of the book:

> Look; under that broad *Beech-tree*, I sate down, when I was last this way a fishing, and the birds in the adjoyning Grove seemed to have a friendly contention with an Eccho, with an Eccho whose dead voice seemed to live in a hollow tree, near to the brow of that Primrose-hill; there I sate viewing the silver-streams glide silently towards their center, the tempestuous Sea; yet, sometimes opposed by rugged roots, and pebble stones, which broke their waves, and turned them into foam: and sometimes I beguil'd time by viewing the harmless Lambs, some leaping securely in the cool shade, whilst others sported themselves in the chearful Sun: and saw others craving comfort from the swoln Udders of their bleating Dams. As I thus sate, these and other sights had so fully possest my soul with content, that I thought as the Poet has happily exprest it:
>
> > *I was for that time lifted above earth;*
> > *And possest joys not promis't in my birth.*
> > (*Angler*, 231; the "Poet" has not been identified.)

The scene, and the conversation, are typical of Walton's golden world, no more particularly descriptive, in this case of England, than are other conventionally depicted literary paradises.

The Compleat Angler is an eclectic work that brings together the georgic and pastoral modes and uses also a dialogue form—a decisive point about this work of varied intentions, for Walton's designs are as complex and mixed as the several forms to which he is indebted. The dialogue around which Walton develops his book certainly serves his purpose well; it provides a freshness and a sense of intimacy, and the dramatic quality ideally suits its instructional and didactic intentions. This mode of easy question and answer, with long interpretive discourses, seems so inevitably part of *The Compleat Angler* that most readers would not realize how keen is Walton's artfulness. The dialogue form is well known in classical literature, having been put to a variety of uses in works that range from the philosophic works of Plato to the satires of Lucian; but it was most familiar in Walton's time as a means for carrying on political or religious controversy, as with the Marprelate tracts at the end of the sixteenth century or with often ephemeral documents upholding or condemning the Laudian "reforms" of Charles I's reign. The tone of these works is nearly always brash, irritable, stubborn, impudent—characteristics utterly alien to Walton's amiable and good-natured dramatic dialogue. During this period, books of instruction, like *The Compleat Angler*, also commonly make use of dialogue, but these works are frequently narrow and limited, or sometimes coarse and bad tempered.[9] Yet one early manual, which aims to instruct by means of a dialogue between master and pupil, stands out from the rest. Roger Ascham's *Toxophilus* (1545), about archery, dignifies learning and piety and offers a pleasing model for Walton's *Compleat Angler*, for as one of Walton's most helpful commentators notes, "in each work there is a similar development of the theme, with first a formal debate on the activity that the book is concerned with, next the conversion of the skeptic, and finally the detailed instruction of the convert by the master of the art" (Cooper, 84).

Thus we must recognize that *The Compleat Angler* is difficult for the late-twentieth-century reader, who often seeks some single, cohering principle in any work, to categorize; but Walton's use of different genres or forms, and the variety of his intentions, would have been readily understood by the seventeenth-century audience. That the book has appealed to so many different readers—and readerships—over the 300 years since its first publication is clearly demonstrated by its numerous editions; except for a hiatus following Walton's death, the book appears seldom to have been out of print. No common manual on fishing could survive for so long, or in such a way; we have seen, indeed, that other books on angling known to Walton and from which he often borrowed have long been forgotten. Surely Walton has successfully bestowed special wisdom on his book: he is a practical angler, but he is also a charm-

ing companion who teaches good conduct by example, who reflects on
the social and political order, who speaks to the upheavals of his time
but who can universalize his themes.[10]

One need never go near a pond or river or see a fishing line to appreciate Walton's gentle satire and comment on humanity, for Walton
knows how to induce detachment and good affections in his readers. He
writes: "I have found in my self, That the very sitting by the Rivers side,
is not only the fittest place for, but will invite the Anglers to Contemplation: That it is the fittest place, seems to be witnessed by the children
of *Israel*, who having banish'd all mirth and Musick from their pensive
hearts, and having hung up their then mute Instruments upon the Wil-
low trees, growing by the Rivers of *Babylon*, sate down upon those banks
bemoaning the *ruines* of *Sion*, and contemplating their own sad condition" (*Angler*, 70).[11] The immediate reference is to Psalm 137, "By the
waters of Babylon, there we sat down and wept, when we remembered
Zion. On the willows there we hung up our lyres. . . . How shall we sing
the Lord's song in a foreign land?" But the implicit reference is to the
defeated royalists, and to the disestablished church and its alienated
clergy—many of them friends of Walton's. Although the times were
evil, Walton would not have lyres hang unused, for his wish is to
admonish persons to continue to sing no matter the weather, like
Lovelace in "The Grasse-hopper," to enjoy good fellowship wherever it
may be found, and to hope for revival. Such a message is particular, but
it is also obviously comprehensive. Walton urges both contemplation
and positive action.

Walton's genial yet bittersweet message of failure and of hope would
have seemed more persuasive in his own time than it does in ours, and
his oblique commentary on the eclipse of the royalist cause, which in the
early 1650s must have appeared as the beginning of an interminable
darkness, was deeply significant to his contemporaries. He evidently
intends a pun on the title of his fishing manual: *The Compleat Angler* is a
comprehensive work for anglers who care for the *Anglicana Ecclesia*—the
Church of England. Although *Anglican* was not to become a usual term
for an adherent of the English church until the early nineteenth century,
the word commonly described the institution and its episcopal organization in Walton's day. He seems to have intended "Anglican" in this
sense, just as William Laud was to define it for King James in his famous
"conference" with the Jesuit Fisher in 1622; or as John Cosin in such
Caroline documents as his "State of us who adhere to the Church of
England," or his Latin tracts on the faith, discipline, and sacred rites of

the Anglican Church ("De Ecclesiae Anglicanae"); or especially as Richard Mountague was to state so boldly in his celebrated *Appello Caesarem* (1625), in which he defines the historic Church of England: *"The* VISIBLE CHURCH *of* CHRIST *is a congregation of faithfull men, in which the pure Word of* GOD *is preached, and the Sacraments be duely ministred."* Mountague continues in a fashion typical of the attitudes that Walton would have heard again and again and to which he heartily assented, that "the [Anglican] Church is *invisible* in her more noble parts. . . . POPERY is for *Tyranny*, PURITANISME for *Anarchy* . . . both alike enemies unto Piety."[12] But the Anglican way is, like angling, most likely to lead toward peaceableness and propriety, and Walton reflects this serenity in *The Compleat Angler*, however much he means implicitly to castigate antiroyalists, nonconformists, and opponents of the rightful Church of England. Walton retains the poise of Anglican (and angling) harmony throughout his most famous book, and except for some scornful complaint in the *Life of Sanderson*, he rarely comments directly on the political and ecclesiastical upheavals of his age.[13]

   The Compleat Angler, like Burton's *Anatomy of Melancholy*, was frequently revised, each edition growing in length and in detail, but the fifth edition of 1676—the last published in Walton's lifetime—retains almost all of the material of the first edition of 1653; the last more fully develops all of the features already described, especially the georgic and pastoral modes. The dialogue is also fuller, and the book is supplemented by more poems, songs, and engravings of the various fish being discussed and is generally more richly furnished. It is this "final" author's version that has usually been reprinted, sometimes bound with an additional part (in fact a separate work) by Charles Cotton (a third part by Robert Venables appeared also in the edition of 1676 but not in subsequent editions); this is the version that we shall now more closely examine.

Plan of the Work

Walton begins with three men who are traveling north along the road that follows the Lea valley from Tottenham to Ware, in Hertfordshire: Piscator, an angler, Venator, a hunter, and Auceps, a faulkner (the Latin names of course designate the several vocations). Venator wants to go to the Thatched House in Hoddesdon (an actual inn), which lies 12 miles farther than Tottenham; but Auceps plans to leave the road some miles before Tottenham and go toward Theobalds. The route, the places, and the characters are thus defined, and so the company walks forth on an early May morning, Piscator having overtaken the others and opened the cheerful "conference." "We are all so happy as to have a fine, fresh, cool morning," Venator says, "and I hope we shall each be the happier in the others company." Auceps rejoins, "I will be free and openhearted, as discretion will allow me to be with strangers" (*Angler*, 174).

Each of these affable journeyers offers a description and a defense of his occupation. Both Venator and Auceps at first are inclined to scoff at Piscator, the "simple" angler, but the latter is ready to hear how well the others can justify their pursuits. For the time being, Piscator is content to answer Venator's specific charge that the angler's recreation belongs to "simple men." Piscator acknowledges his own simplicity,

> if by that you mean a harmlesness, or that simplicity which was usually found in the primitive Christians, who were (as most Anglers are) quiet men, and followers of peace; men that were so simply-wise, as not to sell their Consciences to buy riches, and with them vexation and a fear to die; If you mean such simple men as lived in those times when there were fewer Lawyers; when men might have had a Lordship safely conveyed to them in a piece of Parchment no bigger than your hand, (though several sheets will not do it safely in this wiser age) I say Sir, if you take us Anglers to be such simple men as I have spoke of, then my self and those of my profession will be glad to be so understood: But if by simplicity you meant to express a general defect in those that profess and practise the excellent Art of Angling, I hope in time to disabuse you, and make the contrary appear so evidently, that if you will but have patience to hear me, I shall remove all the Anticipations that discourse, or time, or prejudice have possess'd you with against that laudable and ancient art; for I know it is worthy the *knowledge* and *practise* of a wise man. (*Angler*, 178–79)

Walton plainly identifies with Piscator and speaks through him, and here, as elsewhere, with ironic glancing at the current (but perennial) abuses of his time. Piscator, in order to demonstrate his patience for hearing the views of his companions, lets them speak at length. Because Piscator is so confident that his own recreation is far superior to theirs, he is happy to wait for the last word, which is bound to be most weighty and rhetorically effective. It will in fact occupy most of this very long first chapter of *The Compleat Angler*.

The curious debate over the advantages of different pastimes seems to recall in a general way discussions of the natural elements in tradi-

The Compleat Angler or the Contemplative man's Recreation.

Being a Difcourfe of

FISH and FISHING,

Not unworthy the perufal of moft *Anglers.*

Simon Peter *faid, I go a* fifhing *: and they faid, We alfo wil go with thee.* John 21.3.

London, Printed by *T. Maxey* for RICH. MARRIOT, in *S. Dunftans* Churchyard Fleetftreet, 1653.

ENGRAVED TITLE PAGE OF THE FIRST EDITION OF *THE COMPLEAT ANGLER* (1653).

From the Hawthorn Collection in the Woodward Library, University of British Columbia, Vancouver.

tional works on natural history, such as appear in Pliny. Auceps the faulkner, the lover of hawks, is first to enlarge on his vocation. He speaks eloquently of the element of air in which he trades, and he invokes colorful scenes of the lark, blackbird, and nightingale, which make celestial music. Besides all of this remarkable music, birds are useful—some can carry letters, bring news (like the dove that returned to Noah)—and the Holy Spirit himself took the shape of a dove. Venator next takes his turn in commendations of the earth that supports the hunter: "What more manly exercise than *hunting the Wild Bore*, the *Stag*, the *Buck*, the *Fox* or the *Hare?*" (*Angler*, 184–85). Health, strength, and activity are stimulated. Venator cuts his speech short so that Piscator will have time for an "easy" discourse, though doubtless a "watry" one. Piscator explains his motives and beliefs, which are fundamental to the whole of *The Compleat Angler*, for like all anglers he must be concerned with "calm and quiet": "We seldome make the Welkin to roar, we seldom take the name of God into our mouths but it is either to praise him or pray to him; if others use it vainly in the midst of their recreations, so vainly as if they meant to conjure, I must tell you, it is neither our fault nor our custom; we, we protest against it. But, pray remember I accuse no body; for as I would not make a *watry* discourse, so I would not put too much *vinegar* into it; nor would I raise the reputation of my own Art by the diminution or ruine of anothers" (185). So Piscator prefaces his prolonged litany on water and the fish that swim in it, pausing only long enough to bid farewell to Auceps as he turns to make his separate way to Theobalds. Yet he parts from Piscator and Venator "full of good thoughts," especially about angling. Walton thus reminds us that we are still walking, conversing, and starting to learn that angling is an art of antiquity, "and an Art worthy the knowledg and practise of a wise man" (189). Venator, who seems ready to forget about hunting, begs to hear more, and to become Piscator's student, or "scholar," and become instructed in it.

But angling—as ancient as Deucalion's flood—cannot be learned by anyone but those who are born to it, or who would want sincerely to try to develop the right disposition: "[H]e that hopes to be a good *Angler* must not only bring an inquiring, searching, observing wit; but he must bring a large measure of hope and patience, and a love and propensity to the Art it self; but having once got and practis'd it, then doubt not but *Angling* will prove to be so pleasant, that it will prove to be like Vertue, *a reward to it self*" (*Angler*, 190). On the old controversy of whether happiness consists more in contemplation or in action, Piscator (Walton) would forbear to declare himself; nevertheless, he offers a solution by declaring a third opinion, his belief that contemplation and action meet together "and do most properly belong to the most *honest, ingenuous, quiet,* and *harmless* art of *Angling*" (*Angler*, 193).

Now Walton provides a discourse on rivers and on some varieties of fish, with a conclusion chosen out of George Herbert's "Providence" (stanzas 36, 8, 7; that is, three stanzas, one from the end, two near the beginning), and finally a selection on the creation of fishes from Sylvester's DuBartas (fifth day of the first week, ll. 29–48). One purpose of all this quotation and the effect of the references to anglers from (allegedly) Moses, Job, Amos, Isaiah, and the various apostles is to anticipate and highlight two contemporary portraits. The first is of Alexander Nowell (1511–1601), dean of St. Paul's, whose great age was the result of angling and temperance. Walton describes him as "an honest Angler," who made "that *good, plain, unperplext* Catechism which is printed with our good old Service Book" (that is, the Book of Common Prayer; *Angler*, 203).[14] The identification of devotion, conscientious churchmanship, even sound theology, in a former and better age is almost complete—but there remains the second portrait of Walton's friend Sir Henry Wotton, whose life Walton had two years earlier published with *Reliquiae Wottonianae*. Now Wotton is employed for displaying that necessary conjunction of contemplation and action that angling provides: "the vertue of Humility . . . a calmness of spirit, and a world of other blessings attending upon it" (205–6). This impressive (and very long) first chapter of *The Compleat Angler* ends with a selection of verse from Wotton and from John Dennys, *The Secrets of Angling* (1613), which show the happiness of undisturbed minds. Piscator and Venator, now at the end of their journey, arrive at the Thatched House ready to refresh themselves with a drink and some rest. They look forward to the next days when Piscator will demonstrate the angling art that he has so persuasively celebrated.

In the remaining 20 chapters of this sixth edition of *The Compleat Angler*, Walton leads his two characters on a number of separate or occasional day excursions, often beginning and ending the day evidently in the same (or a very similar) lodging but apparently moving south toward Tottenham, where the initial meeting took place, in the direction of London. Walton's most obvious purpose in the first, much shorter edition of only 13 chapters was to give instruction in fishing; now the increased size of the book allows not only for instruction but also for explanation of the habits of the various fish, for digressions on natural history, and for extended moralizing and "merriment." We begin with the enemies of fish, especially the otter, and the ruinous habits of the cormorant, the bittern, the osprey, the sea gull; of the swan, goose, and duck; and of the unpleasant water rat, "against all which any honest man may make a just quarrel, but I will not, I will leave them to be quarrelled with, and kill'd by others; for I am not of a cruel nature, I love to kill nothing but Fish" (*Angler*, 214).

Of the fish that Walton discusses, the chub is first—though the order does not seem vital to the development of the book: trout, grayling, pike, carp, bream, tench, perch, eel ("and other fish that want scales"), barbel, gudgion, roach, dace, penk, loach, and bullhead, "some other inferiour Fish," and anything else that can be remembered. Piscator's desire is to be thorough, to omit no species of fish that his companion might discover somewhere in the rivers of England. Such a book ought to become awkward and repetitious, with little coherence; yet *The Compleat Angler* possesses variety and careful patterning, and certain principles of organization, among which are the management of time, movement, and space.

Walton imagines the action of his book to take place during an outdoor ramble toward a certain destination and over a period of several days. The walking and fishing are interrupted by intervals of rest, in shady places by river banks or near meadows, the habitation of lambs and sheep, or else in cheerful and well-managed inns with genial, well-informed landlords or hostesses who know how to dress a fish. Walton's tone is consistently equable, his outlook determinedly old fashioned and nostalgic; in general he is optimistic about the world and its inhabitants, who are ever courteous and live in an idealized social order in which egalitarianism is the rule. Walton of course has adopted a persona in the figure of Piscator, a technique that provides the author with sufficient detachment so that he is able to write his book as a kind of imagined narrative, something quite different from a mere manual on angling.

Walton's depiction of time within this narrative framework is fashioned in several ways. While the action is told in the present tense, we are aware of a past time when living was more crude and less perfect. We travel from place to place; we begin days in freshness and vigor and end them with fatigue born from accomplishment and accompanied by satisfaction. Yet another feature of Walton's fictional time occurs during the various fishing excursions in which Piscator shows Venator what to do, and then, as if in a dramatic change or shift of scene, we realize that an action has occurred and time has suddenly passed. In showing Venator how to fish for the chub, Piscator says, "Go your way presently, take my Rod, and do as I bid you, and I will sit down and mend my tackling till you return back" (*Angler*, 220). Venator replies:

> Truly, my loving Master, you have offered me as fair as I could wish. I'le go and observe your directions.
>
> Look you, Master, what I have done, that which joys my heart, caught just such another *Chub* as yours was.
>
> *Pisc.* Marry, and I am glad of it: I am like to have a towardly Scholar of you. I now see, that with advice and practice you will make an *Angler* in a short time. Have but a love to it and I'le warrant you.

Directions are given, a fish is caught, appreciation is rendered, and the next lesson on baiting is offered.

In the following chapter, chapter 4, "Observations of the nature and breeding of the Trout; and how to fish for him," Piscator and Venator are trout fishing. After elaborately describing the habits of the trout, the former declares that he will demonstrate his skill in catching one, and then "at my next walking either this evening, or to morrow morning I will give you direction, how you your self shall fish for him" (*Angler*, 230). Venator replies in such a way that we may assume movement and understand the implicit action:

> Trust me, Master, I see now it is a harder matter to catch a *Trout* than a *Chub:* for I have put on patience, and followed you these two hours, and not see a Fish stir, neither at your Minnow nor your Worm.
>
> *Pisc.* Well Scholar, you must endure worse luck sometime, or you will never make a good Angler. But what say you now? there is a *Trout* now, and a good one too, if I can but hold him, and two or three turns more will tire him: Now you see he lies still, and the sleight is to land him: Reach me that Landing Net: So (Sir) now he is mine own, what say you now? is not this worth all my labour and your patience?

Again, the narrative is dramatic and lively, reflecting in the present mode activity as if onstage—only bracketed directions to the actors are omitted, but they are assumed.

Walton manipulates narrative time skillfully, and simultaneously he arranges the materials in *The Compleat Angler* so that we feel an action is unfolding inevitably, not in a haphazard or loosely episodic manner. This impression seems justified even though the presentation of the different kinds of fish seems arbitrary, nor is there usually a clear sense of proceeding from easy to difficult lessons; for if the hardest were to be saved for last, then trout fishing, with the complicated procedures for making bait and artificial flies, should come much later in the book—not in the first third. But Walton is cleverly distributing his materials in a way that defies conventional expectations. One may see this point illustrated by the introduction of the milkmaid's and her mother's song at the end of the first chapter on trout fishing, from which I have just quoted.

The songs are "smooth"; the first one, sung by the milkmaid, is the familiar "Come live with me, and be my Love, / And we will all the pleasures prove"; the second song by the milkmaid's mother is the answer, "If all the world and Love were young, / And truth in every Shepherds tongue." Walton attributes these verses to Marlowe and Ralegh, respectively, who are supposed traditionally to be their authors. The mother tells us that she learned the first song when she was young—her daughter's age. But she sings the second song, which fits her mood better now; for during the past two or three years "the cares of the World began to take hold of me." The anglers shall hear them both, and Piscator, who seems to have heard them on an earlier occasion, is happy for this musical and poetic diversion: "They were old fashioned Poetry, but choicely good, I think much better than the strong lines that are now in fashion in this critical age" (*Angler*, 232–35). Does Walton mean Piscator's words to refer to anyone in particular? They might, as Anthony Low reminds us, recall the common application of the phrase "strong lines" to "metaphysical poetry," especially to poets like John Donne. These songs seem, in the way that they appear so easily in *The Compleat Angler*, to spring from "a rustic oral tradition . . . remnants of a more gracious age of song, which still persists in the memory of a few men and women who survive from that better time."[15]

If Donne is tacitly invoked at this point in the narrative, there is no appropriate way to quote from him. *His* answer to Marlowe's song is the witty, "strong-lined" "The Baite," which begins innocently and in the same pastoral mode, but in Donne's hands it becomes a dark and dismissive world. Yet "The Baite" does indeed appear much later in *The Compleat Angler*, and an attentive reader will not have forgotten the previous songs of the milkmaid and her mother to which Donne's lines obviously allude. This time Venator, not Piscator, says that he will recite "a Copy of Verses that were made by Doctor *Donne*, and made to shew the world that he could make soft and smooth Verses when he thought smoothness worth his labour; and I love them the better, because they allude to Rivers, and fish and fishing" (*Angler*, 313). But Venator misses the point, for although Donne begins with the usual "Come live with me, and be my Love," he soon mocks the pastoral world and plays with its conventions. Nor is "The Baite" a song like the poems it parodies; it is a contemporary text by a "modern" poet. Walton must be aware of Donne's purpose, for he seems to use this poem as an ironic comment on his own ideal of the civilized and social world. Such subtle echoing is characteristic of Walton's highly sophisticated composition.[16] Piscator's response is to turn away from Donne to observations of the eel.

Walton's book is full of variety, as we have seen, and much deliberately ordered digression, for everything has its proper place, whether immediately apparent or not. The chapter on eels "and other fish that want scales" follows the recital of Donne's witty and subversively unpastoral poem; we may fancy, perhaps without overinvention, that Walton is turning to less attractive, or less familiar, fish in the remaining pages of the book, which are, in any case, well flavored with amusement and advice. Walton is always an accomplished provider of detailed instructions; along with information about the culture of fish and fishing, he intersperses recipes for fit preparations of one's catch. Some of these recipes appear to have been borrowed or adapted from various manuals or cookbooks; but some, like the recipe for roasting the eel, is Walton's own:

> First, wash him in water and salt, then pull off his skin below his vent or navel, and not much further: having done that, take out his guts as clean as you can, but wash him not: then give him three or four scotches with a knife, and then put into his belly and those scotches, sweet herbs, an Anchovy, and a little Nutmeg grated or cut very small, and your herbs and Anchovis must also be cut very small, and mixt with good butter and salt; having done this, then pull his skin over him all but his head, which you are to cut off, to the end you may tie his skin about that part where his head grew, and it must be so tyed as to keep all his moisture within his skin: and having done this, tie him with Tape or Pack-thred to a spit, and rost him leasurely, and baste him with water and salt till his skin breaks, and then with Butter: and having rosted him enough, let what was put into his belly, and what he drips be his sawce. (*Angler*, 319)

Piscator seems eager here, as with his other recipes, to urge the best means of preparing fish, means that are most effective and also most traditional.

The final chapter provides more recipes, these for making and dyeing fishing line, but in the last paragraphs there are general formulas for living well. Walton gives his characters *sententiae* to speak, moral wisdom for reflection, and resolutions that summarize and conclude the whole work. As they approach Tottenham High-Cross, Piscator muses to his companion:

> I will . . . in the cool shade of this sweet *Hony-suckle-Hedg,* mention to you some of the thoughts and joys that have possest my Soul since we two met together. . . .
> Well Scholar, I have almost tir'd my self, and I fear more than almost tir'd you: but I now see *Tottenham High-Cross,* and our short walk thither shall put a period to my too long discourse, in which, my meaning was, and is, to plant that in your mind, with which I labour to possess my own Soul: that is; a meek and thankful heart. . . . Therefore my advice is, that you *endeavour to be honestly rich; or, contentedly poor.* (*Angler,* 362, 365 – 66)

Venator is thankful "for all your good directions," and he commends now a little rest in a shady arbor, which will secure them both from the heat of the sun and from an approaching shower. They shall enjoy a drink made of sack, milk, oranges, and sugar—"a drink like *Nectar,* indeed too good for any body but us *Anglers*" (366 – 67). And there is a toast, and a pledge to friendship, with the recitation of verses by Sir Henry Wotton. *The Compleat Angler* is moving quietly to its close, with the scriptural blessing pronounced by Piscator, the guiding principle (from 1 Thessalonians 4:11) of the whole book: *"Study to be quiet."*

Chapter Five
Walton's Fame and Influence

Except for the period from 1676 to 1750, Walton's works have always been in print. Sometimes the *Lives* were especially renowned, sometimes *The Compleat Angler* was preeminent. But the unassuming linen draper's reputation has remained constant in a surprising way, and his works have been influential as well as generally fashionable. His readers have included notable writers, illustrators, and churchmen, and a review of this widespread esteem provides a fascinating study of the unfolding history of Walton's work. This chapter will attempt to trace his reputation through the observations made by writers and critics in the years since the first publication of the *Life of Donne,* in 1640. Writing at the end of the nineteenth century, James Russell Lowell remarked with the kind of affection common to Walton criticism that "He left behind him two books, each a masterpiece in its own simple and sincere way, and only the contemplative leisure of a life like his could have secreted the precious qualities that assure them against decay. . . . Of the outward husk of this life we know comfortably little, but of the kernel, much, and that chiefly from such unconscious glimpses as he himself has given us."[1]

The Earliest Editions

During Walton's lifetime there were five editions of *The Compleat Angler:* in 1653, 1655, 1661 (with a second issue in 1664), 1668, and 1676. The *Lives of Donne* (1640, 1658), *Wotton* (1651, 1654), *Hooker* (1665, 1666), and *Herbert* (1670) were collected, augmented, or revised, in 1670 and 1675. Individual *Lives* were printed in separate editions of their subjects' works, and thus Hooker's biography appears as a prefix to every complete edition of his *Works* from 1665 onward, although Walton's authorship is not always acknowledged. The *Life of Sanderson* was published in 1678 and 1681.

Critical responses to Walton's near-obsessive concern for so much revision has taken a variety of forms. F. G. P. Kellendonk remarks (and the numerous editions already cited prove) that Walton was continuously revising his work "very scrupulously."[2] But Walton was aiming for clarification in this process of revision, and according to Judith Anderson, he "does not hesitate to change a word--anyone's word—if he thinks he can make a passage clearer, less ambiguous or better,—that is, true. Walton revises habitually, but virtually never does he restore earlier readings."[3] Steven Zwicker regards Walton's additions to his work over his long life as "an art of assemblage."[4] And John Butt contends that "Walton found some difficulty in expression and in satisfying himself with what he had written."[5] H. J. Oliver sees the purpose of Walton's revisions in another light: "Walton was anxious to reinforce what we might call its moral value, and avoid any suspicion of lightmindedness. . . . He also takes the opportunity of making further reflexions on the follies of the day."[6] Anderson, in commenting on the *Life of Donne*, observes that "the very fact of Walton's three versions [of this *Life*] suggests his purpose . . . evolved, becoming sharper and clearer over a period of about thirty-five years. His finished portrait of Donne, as his contemporary [Charles] Cotton recognizes, is an honorific memorial and, quite literally a monumental work of art" (Anderson, 57).

In both his *Lives* and *The Compleat Angler*, Walton writes as a faithful Anglican, even though *Donne* and *Wotton* and the *Angler* were all published during the Interregnum at a time of extraordinary political and ecclesiastical upheaval, when episcopacy was banished and use of the Prayer Book illegal. Prudence and enlightened self-interest prevented him from being outspoken in the early 1640s and 1650s, but he was able to speak quite openly in later editions, when the monarchy and church had been restored. In discussing the various versions of *The Compleat Angler*, B. D. Greenslade observes, "In writing of angling Walton was concerned to please those whom he respected most, and . . . in the unhappiest days of the Church he was offering them something of his own."[7] Later, when all was much safer, Walton could write of Hooker as if he were providing a history of the church, and Butt correctly sees that for Walton "Sanderson became synonymous with the Puritan struggles in Charles I's reign and the Church's evil days in the Commonwealth period. . . . Walton [was] writing both from personal experience and from the experience of Bishop Morley at his elbow."[8]

John Buchan, in his 1901 introduction to his edition of *The Compleat Angler*, records that in Walton's own day "the single dissentient voice in the chorus of praise [for Walton] was that of Richard Franck, the Cromwellian soldier, who, having a taste for rough and moorland waters, had little patience with Walton's gentle pastoral."[9] Franck published *Northern Memoirs,* of which Sir Walter Scott, who edited the work and whose publishing house produced it, wished that Walton, "who had a true eye for nature . . . had made this northern tour instead of Franck, and had detailed in the beautiful simplicity of his Arcadian language his observations on the scenery and manners of Scotland" (Buchan, xvii). Of course, Franck was the first to describe in detail the art of fishing for salmon, as opposed to Walton's angling for trout, as we learn from Nigel Smith:

> Much of the information contained in *Northern Memoirs* is concerned with Scottish fishing, and Scottish towns and countryside—the reason for Scott's interest. . . . Different knowledges, cosmologies, pieties, and political visions, produce in Franck a deep resistance to Walton, despite his own respect for the literary achievement of *The Compleat Angler* and his humility. . . . Franck considered Walton's knowledge to be inferior to his own, and derived from books rather than angling experience. . . . This opinion was based not only on a reading of *The Compleat Angler*, but also . . . upon an encounter between the two men.[10]

Walton and Franck had met at Stafford and debated the breeding of pickerel. Walton, it seems, turned away angrily when he did not get the better of the argument, according to Franck's account of it—the only one we have. The intriguing fact is that they disagreed not only about the breeding of pickerel and how to write about angling but also about religion, for Franck was an outspoken Puritan who supported Cromwell. Yet their views were not altogether opposed, for the final section of Franck's work resembles Walton's insofar as the species of fish are described and angling advice given (Smith, 60). Smith hails Franck's work as "a Commonwealth radical's response to the Restoration," which actually reveals Walton's influence; Walton could have had no notion when he wrote *The Compleat Angler* that he would arouse such opposition.

Nor might Walton have supposed that his *Lives* would become so celebrated. John Dryden, for example, described nonconformity in his preface to *Religio Laici* (1682) by turning to Walton's *Life of Hooker* and to Cranmer's letter, appended to the *Life*. And Anthony à Wood constructed his memoir of Hooker for the *Athenae Oxoniensis* (1698) largely from Walton's *Life*, paying homage to Walton's labors by adding a sketch of Walton's own life to that of Hooker. His own memoir of Hooker is directly followed by one of Cranmer, which hardly seems coincidental.[11]

The Eighteenth Century

The early eighteenth century was a low point in the publication of Walton, with no new editions except for the occasional *Life* attached to some other non-Walton work. Although the *Life of Hooker* was included with Hooker's *Works*, Walton was not identified as its author until the edition of 1705. The lives of Donne and Herbert were also included in various publications of their works. No edition of *The Compleat Angler* appeared until Samuel Johnson encouraged a new edition of the works of "one of his favourite authors" (according to Boswell, he thought so well of Walton's *Compleat Angler* that he included it in a list compiled for the Reverend M. Astle of Ashbourne, in Derbyshire, who wanted to know what books an educated gentleman should read).[12] Moses Browne, however, was to become the editor—not Dr. Johnson—and he gives implicit credit to him as the originator of the idea of a new edition of the *Angler* by saying that his task was begun "at the Instigation of an ingenious and learned Friend, whose Judgment of Men and Books is sufficiently established, by his own Writing, in the Opinion of the World."[13] Little did he realize that his publication would eventually lead to a tedious controversy.

Browne (1704–1787) was a London pen cutter by trade, who eventually took orders but was also an occasional poet, dramatist, and essayist whose work appeared erratically in Edward Cave's *Gentleman's Magazine*. He was also an enthusiastic angler. One of Browne's works was *Piscatory Eclogues*, prefaced by an essay in which he commended Walton's *Angler*. Dr. Johnson seemed to think that Browne's literary experience and his apparent love of angling made him uniquely capable of providing a new edition of Walton's work. In his prefatory remarks Browne praises Walton:

> *The Compleat Angler* of the celebrated Mr *Walton* which . . . I have the pleasure of restoring in the present Manner to the Publick, has been always held in the greatest Reputation, not only by those who have a Relish for the Recreation it treats of, but by all others of different Inclinations who have ever read it, and are the least discerning in Works of *Merit* and *Nature*. Its suitable, elegant Simplicity of Stile, its lively and masterly Descriptions, the most curious Discoveries (for its Time) in Matters of philosophical and historical Science, the happiest Mixture of religious and moral Instruction, enlivened with a Vein of innocent Humour, and chearful Entertainment, appear in every Page of it. Nothing can be drawn more in Character; the honest Man, the plain, good-natured, indifferent

Angler, is conversing with you in every Line; and there is a Modesty so
winning through the Whole; in a rich Store of Learning, it expresses,
under a designed and studied Concealment, that I question if its Equal is
to be met with in any Book (with so unpromising a Title) that has been
written in our language. (Browne, iii)

Basing his text of 1750 on Walton's fourth edition (1668), he added a
number of occasional notes and, according to Bertram Davis, a recent
commentator, "took extraordinary liberties with Walton's text, not
merely by omitting parts of it but, more seriously, by occasionally altering passages—including the poetry—to suit the editor's rather than the
author's taste." Yet Browne had claimed that his emendations were simply a filing "off that Rust, which Time fixes on the most curious and finished Things."[14]

John Hawkins, a younger friend of Dr. Johnson who became his first
biographer and the executor of his will, undoubtedly foresaw difficulties.
He was unhappy with Browne's alterations, and when he heard in 1759
that another edition was in preparation, he offered Browne material that
he himself had gathered for an edition. He also suggested that Browne
use the fifth edition of 1676, the one closest to its author's final intentions. But Browne made only a few changes in his new edition, for the
most part repeating what he had done previously. Recognizing that his
suggestions to Browne had been futile, Hawkins determined to issue a
different and "proper" edition of the *Angler*, which he completed and
published in 1760, just nine months after Browne's second edition.
Hawkins's publisher advertised this text as "A New and Correct Edition," but Browne waded into print in defense of his own edition along
with an attack on Hawkins. After several of Browne's vicious diatribes
appeared in various publications, Hawkins at last replied, making com-
parisons between his own and Browne's text in such a way that Browne,
fearing ridicule, finally was quiet. "To do as Browne did," writes
Bertram Davis, "was to convey to the public not the text which Walton
wrote, but the text which Browne would have wished him to write had
Walton been attempting to please a mid-eighteenth century audience
such as Browne conceived it to be" (Davis, 102).

Hawkins wrote in the introduction to his 1760 edition: "All that the
editor requests in return for the pains he has taken is, that the reader
will do him the justice to believe that his only motives for the republication of this work were a desire to perpetuate the memory of a meek,
benevolent, pious man, and to contribute something to the improve-

ment of an art of which he professes himself a lover" (Buchan, x). Browne again brought out a further edition in 1772, taking, as Buchan pointed out in 1901, "scandalous liberties with the text . . . in general [representing] the worst editorial tradition" (xv). As time would show, Hawkins emerged the victor in this controversy, for as Buchan continues: "Sir John Hawkins in 1760 prepared a much more valuable reprint. His edition is still the main fount of our biographical material as far as the authors are concerned for he drew upon the researches of the famous antiquarian [William] Oldys, the Norroy King-of-Arms" (Buchan, xv).

Dr. Johnson's first recorded comment about Hawkins's edition is from 1774, when Johnson was corresponding with the Reverend Dr. George Horne about the *Lives*, and it perhaps explains why Johnson never "obliged the Publick" with his own biography of Walton: "The Life of Walton has happily fallen into good hands. Sir John Hawkins has prefixed it to the late edition of the Angler, very diligently collected, and very elegantly composed. You will ask his leave to reprint it, and not wish for a better" (Davis, 108). As for the dispute between Browne and Hawkins, Dr. Johnson would undoubtedly have shared Hawkins's views (Davis, 105).

But Dr. Johnson urged still another edition of Walton, this time of the *Lives*. On 30 August 1774, Boswell wrote to him from Edinburgh: "It gives me great pleasure to hear that a republication of *Izaak Walton's Lives* is intended" (Boswell, 2:324). This was evidently a project very important to Johnson, for Boswell later writes: "He talked of Izaak Walton's *Lives*, which was one of his favourite books. Dr. Donne's *Life*, he said, was the most perfect of them. He observed that 'it was wonderful that Walton, who was in a very low situation in life, should have been familiarly received by so many great men, and that at a time when the rank of societies were kept more separate than they are now.' He supposed that Walton had then given up his business as a linen-draper and sempster, and was only an author; and added that he was a great panegyrist" (Boswell, 2:417). Two men were considered for this editorial task, but some confusion prevented either from accomplishing it. The first (and Boswell's choice) was Dr. Horne, whom Boswell introduces, as well as Lord Hailes:

> We drank tea with Dr. Horne, late President of Magdalen College, and Bishop of Norwich, of whose abilities, in different respects, the publick has had eminent proofs, and the esteem annexed to whose character was increased by knowing him personally. He had talked of publishing an

edition of Walton's *Lives*, but had laid aside that design, upon Dr. John-son's telling him, from mistake, that Lord Hailes intended to do it. I had wished to negociate between Lord Hailes and him, that one or other should perform so good a work. JOHNSON. "In order to do it well, it will be necessary to collect all the editions of Walton's *Lives*. By way of adapt-ing the book to the taste of the present age, they have, in a later edition, left out a vision which he relates Dr. Donne had, but it should be restored; and there should be a critical catalogue given of the works of the different persons whose lives were written by Walton, and therefore their works must be carefully read by the editor." (Boswell, 2:510)

Without Johnson's intervention, an eighteenth-century edition of the *Lives* did at last emerge in 1796, under the editorship of Thomas Zouch, a prebend of Durham who may be said to have "kidnapped" Walton for the church.

Zouch's ardent wish was to raise a monument on behalf of the High Church tradition, according to Raoul Granqvist's thoughtful analysis, "by reinstituting and securing Walton's divines for her interests":

To Zouch Walton and his divines and the time in which they lived form a single cultural entity, an emblem of an ideal church. The *Lives* embodied for Zouch and his friends the concept of conformism and a tool they could use in current theological polemics. Believing that the unity of the church was threatened by the rise of the Evangelical movement on the one hand, and Chartism on the other, conservative Anglicans took Wal-ton to their hearts.[15]

Zouch's annotated edition would become the one that Dr. Johnson had hoped to do himself, but again according to Granqvist, "it is doubtful whether Johnson, who was an admirer of Walton's skill as a biographer, would have approved of the edition that Zouch turned out. Zouch's massive commentary ignores Walton the artist and the panegyrist. Zouch is preoccupied with treating the biography as contemporary his-tory rather than 'pure history.' Had Johnson edited the work . . . its nineteenth century history would, no doubt, have read differently" (Granqvist, 248). Zouch also edited *Love and Truth* (1680) in 1795 and inserted it into his third edition of the *Lives* (1817) in support of his sense of propriety and conformism. For him Walton's biographies pro-vided Anglican apologists with "a source of theological subtlety and vitality they so badly needed to counter the ecclesiastical biographies published by the Evangelicals and the Roman Catholics. Walton symbolized for them a faith that was not only divine, but palpably human. Zouch's characterization of 'honest Izaak' would be endlessly rehearsed in the century" (Granqvist, 248). Zouch's editions of 1807 and 1817 thus went far to establish the book as a principal Anglican apologetic, and he was the first editor to include a biographical account of Walton himself, emphasizing his piety and his unwavering loyalty to church and king. It is significant that the Society for Promoting Christian Knowledge published Zouch's editions of Walton's *Lives,* for his work seemed to accomplish their founding purposes of instruction, antipopery, augmentation of the repute of Anglicanism, and the devout amusement of the Society's readers.

Romantic and Victorian

During the romantic movement of the earlier nineteenth century, William Wordsworth proved not only an avid reader of Walton's works but also was moved to write a sonnet both on *The Compleat Angler* and on the *Lives.* In 1819 he published one of these sonnets (its composition undated), written on a blank leaf of his copy of *The Compleat Angler:*

> While flowing rivers yield a blameless sport,
> Shall live the name of Walton: Sage benign!
> Whose pen, the mysteries of the rod and line
> Unfolding, did not fruitlessly exhort
> To reverent watching of each still report
> That Nature utters from her rural shrine.
> Meek, nobly versed in simple discipline—
> He found the longest summer day too short,
> To his loved pastime given by sedgy Lee,
> Or down the tempting maze of Shawford brook—
> Fairer than life itself, in this sweet Book,
> The cowslip bank and shady willow-tree;
> And the fresh meads—where flowed, from every nook
> Of his full bosom, gladsome Piety![16]

Walton's writings formed an important part of Wordsworth's most familiar books. Correspondence between himself and Lamb, between

Lamb and Coleridge, and to several other people testify that Walton's writings were very much a part of his ordinary conversation. Writing his "Guide through the District of the Lakes," Wordsworth describes the chevin as a *spiritless* fish, adding in an aside, "(though I am loth to call it so, for it was a prime favourite of Izaak Walton)."[17] Lamb wrote to him on 26 April 1816: "Izaak Walton hallows any page in which his reverend name appears."[18] And in writing a review of Wordsworth's *The Excursion*, Lamb compares the work with Walton's *Angler:* "We breathe in the fresh air, as we do while reading Walton's Complete Angler; only the country about us is much bolder than Walton's, as the thoughts and speculations, which form the matter of the poem, exceed the trifling pastimes and low-pitched conversation of his humble fisherman."[19]

In one of his letters to Mary Wordsworth, written in June 1812 about a proposed holiday, Wordsworth writes, "I hope that Davy will let me have an Angling Rod, and I will take care to bring Izaak Walton."[20] And in a letter in 1816 to an unnamed friend of Robert Burns Wordsworth wrote, "The venerable spirit of Izaak Walton was qualified to have retraced the unsteady course of a highly-gifted man, who, in this lamentable period, and in the versatility of genius, bore no obvious resemblance to the Scottish bard, I mean his friend COTTON—whom, notwithstanding all that the sage must have disapproved of in his life, he honoured with the title of son" (*Prose Works*, 3:120). William Hazlitt, referring to Wordsworth, wrote, "He approves of Walton's Angler, Paley, and some other writers of an inoffensive modesty of pretension."[21]

Lamb mentions Walton at least twice in letters to Coleridge. On 10 June 1796, he writes, "I have just been reading a book which I may be too partial to, as it was the delight of my childhood; but I will recommend it to you: it is Izaak Walton's *Compleat Angler*. All the scientific part you may omit in reading. The dialogue is very simple, full of pastoral beauties, and will charm you. Many pretty old verses are interspersed" (*Works*, 1:586). Later that same year he again takes up the subject in a letter to Coleridge: "Among all your quaint readings did you ever light upon Walton's 'Complete Angler'? I asked you the question once before; it breathes the very spirit of innocence, purity, and simplicity of heart; there are many choice old verses interspersed in it; it would sweeten a man's temper at any time to read it; it would Christianise every discordant angry passion; pray make yourself acquainted with it" (*Letters*, 1:53). There is no reply from Coleridge to Lamb, for all but one of the letters that Coleridge wrote to Lamb during this period have perished, and the remaining letter does not touch on Walton.[22] Yet Coleridge's interest in Walton was well known to the reading public, as was Lamb's and Wordsworth's affection for him (Granqvist, 252n).

When Lamb wrote at length to Robert Lloyd on 7 February 1801, he referred to the better edition of Hawkins:

> I shall expect you to bring me a brimful account of the pleasure which Walton has given you, when you come to town—It must square with your mind. The delightful innocence and healthfulness of the Anglers mind will have blown yours like a Zephyr. —Dont [*sic*] you already feel your spirit *filled* with the scenes?—the banks of rivers—the cowslip beds—the pastoral scenes—the neat alehouses—and hostesses and milk-maids, as far exceeding **Virgil** and **Pope**, as the Holy Living is beyond Thomas a Kempis. —**Are** not the eating and drinking joys painted to the Life?—do they not inspire you with an immortal hunger? ——**Are** not you ambitious of being made an Angler?—What edition have you got? is it **Hawkins's** with plates of Piscator &c? That sells very dear. I have only been able to purchase the last Edition without the old Plates which pleased my childhood;—the plates being worn out, & the old Edition difficult & expensive to procure. —— (The complete Angler is the only Treatise written in Dialogues that is worth a halfpenny.— Many elegant dialogues have been written [such as Bishop Berkley's Minute philoso-pher] but in all of them the Interlocutors are merely abstract arguments personify'd; not living dramatic characters, as in Walton; where *every thing* is *alive;* the fishes are absolutely *charactered;*—and birds and animals are as interesting as men and women.) (*Letters*, 1:270)

In another letter to Robert Lloyd, dated 25 February 1809, he writes, "Of Walton's Angler a new edition is just published with the original plates revived. I think of buying it" (*Letters*, 2:291).

Wordsworth wrote a second sonnet on Walton's *Lives*, which appeared in 1822 in the *Ecclesiastical Sonnets*, as number 3.5 (the third section). The title is Wordsworth's:

Walton's Book of Lives

There are no colours in the fairest sky
So fair as these. The feather, whence the pen
Was shaped that traced the lives of these good Men,
Dropped from an Angel's wing. With moistened eye
We read of faith and purest chastity
In Statesman, Priest, and humble Citizen.

What joy to live, what blessedness to die!

Methinks their very Names shine still and bright

Apart—like glow-worms in the woods of spring,

Or lonely tapers shooting far a light

That guides and cheers—or seen like stars on high,

Satellites burning in a lucid ring

Around meek Walton's heavenly memory.

A twentieth-century editor of these sonnets, Abbie Findlay Potts, observed in her 1922 critical edition that Walton's influence was everywhere evident in them. "Throughout the *Ecclesiastical Sonnets*," she says, "the temper of Walton rules."[23] Moreover, she declares that Milton and Walton had long been the intimate companions of Wordsworth's thought. Summing up the influence Walton exerted on Wordsworth, Potts notes, "Wordsworth's associations, from *Peter Bell* and *Juvenal* on the one hand to Isaak [*sic*] Walton and the acquittal of the Bishops on the other, taught the same lesson throughout his life: the respective value of meek doctrine and transport" (Potts, 210). All the subjects of the *Lives* were important to Wordsworth, including Herbert, with whom he felt a sense of kinship. Potts sees in *Ecclesiastical Sonnet* 2.13 a connection with Walton's account of the Venetian breach with Rome described in the *Life of Sir Henry Wotton;* and in *Ecclesiastical Sonnet* 2.38 she finds an allusion to the *Life of Hooker* (Potts, 255, 273). Writing on 23 March 1846 to an unknown correspondent who was planning to produce an abridgment of Walton's *Life of George Herbert*, Wordsworth observed: "Surely there is no sufficient ground for a feeling that Walton's beautiful performance has not its share of due respect by being treated in this way for such an object as yours. His Book of Lives is matchless and no abridgment of any part of it can make the volume less sought after by those who have the means of procuring it" (*Letters of Wordsworth*, 7:767).

Hazlitt also highly regarded Walton. Interested primarily in *The Compleat Angler*, he wrote an engaging essay about it, depicting its style and predicting its long life:

That well-known work has an extreme simplicity, and an extreme interest, arising out of its very simplicity. In the description of fishing tackle you perceive the piety and humanity of the author's mind. This is the best pastoral in the language not exceeding Pope's or Philips's. . . . He gives the feeling of the open air. We walk with him along the dusty road-side, repose on the banks of the river under a shady tree, and in watching for the finny prey, imbibe what he beautifully calls 'the patience and sim-plicity of poor, honest fishermen.' . . . Good cheer is not neglected in this work. . . . The prints in the *Compleat Angler* give an additional reality and interest to the scenes it describes. While Tottenham Cross shall stand, and longer, thy work, amiable and happy old man, shall last. (Hazlitt, 4:56–57)

Hazlitt, however, remarks on the "cruelty" of fixing a worm on a hook. He excuses Walton by recalling the violence of those times "when they burnt men at a stake 'in conscience and tender heart,' " even beheading their monarch like a common criminal. "Had Walton lived in our day," Hazlitt supposes "he would have been the first to cry out against the cruelty of angling. As it was, his flies and baits were only part of his tackle. *They* had not, at this period, the most distant idea of setting up as candidates for our sympathy! Man is naturally a savage, and emerges from barbarism by slow degrees. Let us take the streaks of light, and be thankful for them, as they arise and tinge the horizon one by one, and not complain because the noon is long after the dawn of refinement" (9:182–83).

Yet another notable admirer of Walton was John Keble, the first modern editor of Hooker's *Works* (1836). In his preface Keble discusses the background to Walton's writing of his *Life of Hooker*, "first written at Archbishop Sheldon's suggestion to correct the errors of that by Bishop Gauden." Keble praises "Walton's veracity, industry, and judgment. The advantage he possessed was great in his connexion with the Cranmer family, Hooker's near neighbours and most intimate friends. . . . [T]he Editor has no wish to deny . . . the peculiar fascination, if one may call it so, by which Walton was led unconsciously to communicate more or less of his own tone and character to all whom he undertook to represent. But this is like his custom of putting long speeches into their mouths: we see at once that it is his way, and it deceives no one."[24]

The outstanding work on Walton's texts and life during the nine-teenth century was done by Sir Nicholas Harris Nicolas. In 1836 he published an edition of *The Compleat Angler* and in the following year *The Lives of Walton and Cotton*. Included in this volume are excerpts from Walton's poetry and details of how Walton came to write his *Lives*. Nicolas quotes from a number of previous biographers to illustrate Wal-ton's character and interests, both religious and political. Writing about the *Angler*, he asserts that this book, "whether considered as a treatise upon the art of Angling, or as a beautiful pastoral, abounding in exquisite descriptions of rural scenery, in sentiments of the purest morality, and in an unaffected love of the Creator and his works, has long ranked amongst the most popular compositions in our language."[25] He provides detailed descriptions of the evolution of the editions that Walton revised during his lifetime, and he identifies Piscator with Walton himself, "for not only does that person express his feelings and opinions, but he adopts his personal acquaintances, and alludes to many circumstances in his own life" (Nicolas, liii). Seven appendices include Walton's entries in his own copy of the Book of Common Prayer, Walton's pedigree, a list of books that he had owned, an account of Walton's charities, and a catalog of portraits of Walton's family. Nicolas also offers a list of Walton's admirers down to his own day, including Dr. Johnson, Scott, Wordsworth, Lady Charlotte Campbell, Wilson the ornithologist, and others. His work closes with the poem written to Walton by Sir Henry Wotton and also with his own reflections about Walton's accomplishments:

> Superior as Walton's intellectual powers undoubtedly were, they sink into nothing when compared with the qualities of his heart; and it is the man, rather than the author, whom his admirers most love to contemplate. No one can read his writings without being impressed with the fervent and unaffected piety, the simplicity of taste, the benevolence of mind, and contentedness of spirit, which are apparent in every thought and expression. In the works of the creation he finds a boundless theme for praise and admiration. Though his wit is rarely brilliant, it never springs from envy or ill-nature; and when truth prevented him from praising the persons of whom he speaks, he is silent, mildly observing that "it becomes him not to censure." (Nicolas, cxxi–cxxii)

We must return to the Zouch editions of Walton's *Lives*, discussed earlier, whose audience was mainly academic and clerical and whose purpose was sectarian and polemical. Zouch did not meet the demands of new readers who were more concerned with the straightforward presentation of the works and their general literary interest. But a new editor and a different kind of edition was to fill this need, and such an edition would become "the matrix" of all subsequent nineteenth-century *Lives*, and more effectively than Zouch would establish Walton and his subjects as principal "cult objects" (Granqvist, 253). John Major was the London bookseller and publisher who edited this new text of the *Lives*,

which first appeared in 1825, following his very popular 1823 edition of
The Compleat Angler—an edition that had 62 later reprints down to
1953. Major's intention was to popularize the *Lives* without concern for
the kind of sectarianism displayed by Zouch. Major did not, however,
include any comprehensive account of Walton's own life, perhaps
assuming that nothing more could or should be added to it, and he thus
gave only a brief sketch of Walton but did add vivid illustrations that
seemed further to secularize his edition. In his edition of the *Lives* that
appeared in 1827, William Dowling provided an enlarged view of Walton's life in which he emphasized Walton's moral earnestness. Major's
edition, now accompanied by Dowling's life, became a commercially
successful book that reached broad sections of the reading public previously unfamiliar with Walton.

   In the midst of Walton's canonization, at least two notable figures
who had profound misgivings about his *Lives* should be mentioned.
Benjamin Hanbury (1778–1864), the nonconformist historian and
Keble's predecessor as editor of Hooker, wrote in 1830 that "the *naivete*
and garrulity of Walton impart a fascination to his narrative, which will
not bear the touch of the disenchanter's rod; for when the veil is with-
drawn, and the smoke of incense is dissipated, we see nothing but the
dregs of credulity and intolerance" (Granqvist, 256). Much earlier, but
in similar fashion, William Warburton (1698–1779), bishop of Gloucester and Pope's executor and editor, had condemned Walton's *Lives* as
"the quaint trash of a fantastical life-writer."[26]

Donne's Preeminence

Throughout this complex history, the reception and influence of Walton's *Life of Donne* stands somewhat apart, probably because of the literary importance and colorful personality of Donne himself. Walton's *Life*
was much admired in his own time, and John Hales's judgment,
reported by Bishop Henry King, may be typical. Hales declared that
"He had not seen a Life written with more advantage to the Subject, or
more reputation to the Writer."[27] Yet Walton's account is misleading in
many details, and its chronology is often confused, facts that stimulated
others to search the original records. Thus in the middle years of the
nineteenth century there appeared, without date, Henry Kent Causton's
"Contemplative Man's Library for the Thinking Few," which included
an edition of *The Life of Donne*, with original notes "by An Antiquary,"
apparently Thomas Edlyne Tomlins, who derived his commentary on

Walton's *Life* from hitherto unsearched sources, such as the archives of
the Ironmongers' Company. Now there began a tradition of two biographies of Donne: Walton's hagiography and antiquarian Tomlins's frag-
mented reconstruction. The two would exist together until the end of
the century, when Augustus Jessopp and Edmund Gosse tried to give a
full and integrated view of Donne (Granqvist, 257).

Two more editions of the *Lives* should be mentioned here, one published by Methuen in 1895 with an introduction by Vernon Blackburn,
who calls Walton "a charming conversationalist and potterer who, fac-
ing Donne, paused with shame upon the threshold of his hero's youthful
fervour"; the other is the Walter Scott Library edition, in which Charles
Hill Dick points to Walton's "rambling style, imprecise documentation,
and silencing of 'Jack Donne' "; he criticizes Walton for being "a man
who was incapable of appreciating so strong and intense an intellect
as Donne's, or of doing justice to an imagination of such calibre"
(Granqvist, 257). Both Jessopp and Gosse attempted to sift out Walton's facts from his anecdotes; Jessopp published his *John Donne* in 1897.
Referring to Walton's *Life*, Jessopp writes:

> It is no panegyric; it is much less a mere dry recital of facts. If, as some
> tell us, poetry is the language of excited feeling, never was there a more
> truly poetic story written than Walton's life of Donne. It is a story told in
> solemn rhythmic prose, throbbing with a burden of tender memories and
> fond regrets too full of blessed associations to allow of any gloom in
> recording them. It is an idealised picture of his master, *famous, calm, and
> dead*, drawn by a disciple who had loved that master with enthusiastic
> loyalty and reverence. . . . Walton could afford to be careless about
> details and accessories when he was setting down the reminiscences of
> others regarding Donne's early life. It seems he could only have known
> him intimately for the five or six years before he died. They were long
> enough, however, to draw together by the mysterious attractive force of
> sympathy the two men of genius who in the circumstances of their lives
> and their education had so little in common. Once brought together in
> close relations, a subtle affinity between the two united them more and
> more closely from day to day.[28]

Two years later, in 1899, Edmund Gosse published the *Life and Letters of
John Donne Dean of St. Paul's*.

Gosse appreciates what Walton has accomplished on Donne's behalf;
he refers to the *Life* "as written for us so charmingly by Izaak Walton."[29]
He does, however, lament the lack of information about Donne's youth:

"Walton, in his exquisite portrait of his friend, has nothing at all to say of the stormy and profane youth which led up to that holy maturity of faith and unction. He chose to ignore or to forget anything which might seem to dim the sacred lustre of the exemplary Dean of St. Paul's" (Gosse, 1:63). He sees Walton's interpretation of the sermon preached on the death of Anne Donne as "too sentimental to be accepted" (2:94), and "an examination of the sermon itself reveals no such emotional or hysterical appeals to sympathy as the sentimental genius of Walton conceived" (2:95). He puzzles over the relationship between Donne and Walton: "We can well understand that when once Donne had come into the circle of Walton's charm of conversation and innocent, brilliant hero-worship, he would not escape from it, but how he was persuaded to enter we shall perhaps never know" (2:254). He evaluates Walton's *Life* and recognizes that it is not, nor ever was intended to be, solely based on fact:

> Walton's monograph expressly deals with the divine life and exemplary death of the Dean, and ought not to be considered as an attempt at a literal picture of his transition through all his ages. It is wilfully and purposely drawn out of focus, the early physical part carefully attenuated, the life of holiness that culminated in a glorious death being no less carefully expanded and emphasised. We do no injustice to Walton in insisting upon this fact, for he would have been the first to acknowledge and to justify it. . . . [O]ne of the most exquisite studies in biographical eulogy which the English language possesses . . . poets and critics of every class have united to praise these exquisite monographs, but no one has qualified the charm of their author more exactly than Wordsworth. (Gosse, 2:317–18)

By the turn of the century, one can see that Walton's *Lives*—at least this one about Donne—were beginning to be viewed with some skepticism.

The fate of one of Walton's most famous stories, that of Donne posing in his shroud, may serve as a concluding reminder of fame's unsteadiness. Dame Helen Gardner dismisses most of the story about Nicholas Stone's remarkable monument of John Donne. She argues at first apologetically: "It seems almost sacrilegious to question the most famous of all the stories about Donne: Walton's account of how he posed when dying for a picture from which the monument in St. Paul's was carved. . . . Walton's account is riddled with inaccuracies."[30] She demonstrates that Donne did indeed give orders that he be painted in his shroud as if ready for burial. But she considers what Walton has fictionalized: "Although I believe that Walton's anecdote of Donne's posing for the monument must be rejected on grounds of its inherent impossibility, I think the story has a core of truth. I think that we should accept that Donne was persuaded . . . that he should have a monument and that he wished to be shown in his shroud, asleep in the Lord and, as his epitaph says, 'looking towards Him whose Name is the Rising.' In order that the sculptor should have a likeness to carve from, he was painted in his shroud either before or just after his death" (Gardner, 44).

American Reception and Foreign Translation

The first edition of *The Compleat Angler* in the United States appeared in 1837. This was the "Tilt edition," printed in London by the publishing house of Charles Tilt, in Edinburgh by J. Menzies, and in Philadelphia by T. Wardle. The second edition with an American imprint was Lippincott's first reprint, in 1844. In 1846, according to the *Dictionary of American Biography*, and in 1847, according to Bernard S. Horne, the first truly American edition was prepared by the Reverend George Washington Bethune (1805–1862), a clergyman of the Dutch Reformed Church, born in New York, educated at Columbia and Princeton, and ordained by the Second Presbytery of New York in 1827. Bethune has recently been described as "beyond question, one of the wisest and most learned of the many wise and learned men who, in the course of three centuries, have provided Walton's masterpiece with appreciative commentary and elucidative notes. . . . Walton and Bethune would never have quarreled over matters of religion, for Bethune made no objection to the Anglican turn that Walton gave the piety which some later editors . . . seem to have found obtrusive."[31] And so the excellent Bethune published what he styled "this darling book" in which the extent of Walton's *Angler* was nearly equaled by that of the editor's introduction and appendix, which contains ballads, music, and papers on American fishing, with the most complete catalog of books on angling ever printed. Yet because of the evident prejudice against the propriety of such a book by a clergyman, Bethune published his edition anonymously.

Another important American edition, notably of the *Lives*, was that of 1889, published with an introduction by James Russell Lowell who, in addition, revised and eliminated some of the notes from the Major editions and added new notes of his own. Lowell wrote a long essay—a brief quotation from it appears at the opening of this chapter—in which he affirms that Walton's "real business in this world was to write the Lives and the 'Complete Angler,' and to leave the example of a useful and unspotted life behind him" (Lowell, 8:82). For Lowell and other American editors, Zouch is the preeminent authority and guide. Thus there is in them all the inclination toward supporting High Church attitudes accompanied by strong dislike of nonconformity. It is remarkable that most of these early American editions of the *Lives* appeared within the 30 years between 1832 and 1866—six in New York and five in Boston—as if mirroring the High Church revival in England.

From the nineteenth century until our own time, Walton has become increasingly well known in non-English-speaking countries, but only recently has *The Compleat Angler* been translated. The first German translation appeared in 1859, then three more German editions were issued, all in 1958. Four editions have appeared in Japan since 1926. An abridged edition was published in French in 1942 with another some 20 years later, followed by an unabridged translation in 1964. Three editions of a Danish translation appeared in 1943, with others following. The first Swedish translation was published in 1945 and the fifth in 1965. The first Finnish edition appeared in 1947.[32]

Walton's *Compleat Angler* has had a still further, less literary history in the United States. In 1922 the Izaak Walton League of America was founded in Chicago by a sportsman named Will Dilg. Dilg, a native of Wisconsin, was devoted to the hobby of fly-fishing and to the outdoor life. He determined to invite like-minded friends to join him in the protection of natural resources in the areas of fish habitat, clean water, and forestry. Walton's name was chosen for the league because he was deemed to have had similar ideals. In calling for conservation from a sportsman's perspective, the Izaak Walton League today numbers 40,000 members who promote a variety of environmental programs. Its members have included Herbert Hoover, who served as honorary president of the league in 1926. Honest Izaak's name continues to live on in unexpected ways.

Contemporary and Enduring Reputation

How may one account for the extraordinary popularity of Walton's writing, above all of *The Compleat Angler*, one of the most reprinted works in English? One of its appeals, especially in the late eighteenth and throughout the nineteenth centuries, springs, as one recent critic astutely remarks, "from its pious and nostalgic evocation of a Jacobean golden world; the book became an icon of contentment for successive generations." Walton seems able in *The Compleat Angler* to articulate social values while avoiding contention and wrangling, an "articulation, though prefaced with disclaimers and surrounded by gestures of artlessness and innocence, is in fact a careful assemblage of stances and tags, of allusions and innuendoes, of symbols and ceremoniousness, of balladry and poetry" (Zwicker, 64, 67).

Hazlitt understood the popularity of the *Angler* quite differently: "The minute descriptions of fishing-tackle, of baits and flies . . . make that work a great favourite with sportsmen: the alloy of an amiable humanity, and the modest but touching descriptions of familiar incidents and rural objects scattered through it, have made it an equal favourite with every reader of taste and feeling" (Hazlitt, 12:26). Elsewhere he declares that *The Compleat Angler* is "full of *naivete*,"

> of unexpected sprightliness, of busy trifling, of dainty songs, of refreshing brooks, of shady arbours, of happy thoughts and of the herb called *Heart's Ease*! Some persons can see neither the wit nor wisdom of this genuine volume, as if a book as well as a man might not have a personal character belonging to it, amiable, venerable for the spirit of joy and thorough goodness it manifests, independently of acute remarks or scientific discoveries: others object to the cruelty of Walton's theory and practice of trout-fishing—for my part, I should as soon charge an infant for killing a fly, and I feel the same sort of pleasure in reading his book as I should have done in the company of this happy, child-like old man, watching his ruddy cheek, his laughing eye, the kindness of his heart, and the dexterity of his hand in seizing his finny prey." (17:155–56)

Hazlitt, who expressed alarm over putting a worm on a hook, was perhaps more naive than Walton, yet his inability to see Walton's deeper intentions remained typical of writers well into this century. For example, Peter Oliver, writing in 1936, calls the *Angler* "a dear and much loved book." Trying to explain Walton's perennial attractiveness, he ponders qualities that have sustained the popularity of other writers: "He was no poet, no prophet; his was no tortured soul . . . he used no force to spread his message, but so well he knew its sweetness that he could let it commend itself to the hearts of men. He is no wanderer with a hungry heart, and though each page of him is full of inspiration, his yearning was nobler than suffering."[33] In a similar way, John Buchan wrote a summary of Walton's influence down to the beginning of this century:

In his own day, and in later times, Walton has been the mark for a eulogy which has scarcely been given to any other Englishman short of the very greatest. To Drayton he was his "honest old friend." To Cotton he was a "second father," a master in angling. . . . In the next century Johnson led the way in appreciation by saying that "he considered the preservation and elucidation of Walton a pious work." . . . So, too, Charles Lamb . . . Sir Walter Scott . . . Wordsworth. . . . To Byron, who was no fisher and not even a well-wisher, he is merely the "quaint old cruel coxcomb"; and to Leigh Hunt, himself the most effeminate of men, he is something of the old woman. Among later appreciations we need only mention Mr. Lang's graceful epistle . . . and Mr. Lowell's acute and interesting essay. . . . The *Angler* has been so praised for centuries that a modern writer must refrain from eulogy and seek only the bare phrases of justice. . . . [I]t is easy to look on the work merely as a quaint medley, and forget that in its own day it was a most valuable treatise on the practice of the art, and that still it is not wholly superseded. (Buchan, xvii, xix)

Such judgments as these lead one to view Walton as a simple fisherman, offering homespun philosophy along with tips on angling. Walton's *Lives*, however, have generally been spared such sentimental criticism. One almost sees a different writer who is subtle and discriminating. In writing his *Life of Donne*, Judith Anderson commends as "responsible and impressive" Walton's "use of documents, his awareness of narrative chronology, his care, when possible, to employ phrases that Donne created, instead of those entirely of his own invention, and his frequent indications of his own sources and procedures" (Anderson, 52). These are not traits that one would necessarily associate with Walton, but his desire for studious inquiry is further urged by John Butt, who claims that "Walton had the intelligence necessary for research. His use of records corroborates this" (Butt, 77). Walton certainly relied greatly on many source books, sometimes quoting at considerable length and without acknowledgment.[34] But Walton must not be held accountable to the standards of the modern historian; he was determined to dramatize events whenever that would help to give an essential picture of a life— factual history is not so much Walton's concern as is "the perceptive truth of his synthesis and, indeed, of his fiction" (Anderson, 61). His scriptural quotations, which are often quite inaccurate, simply reveal the inclination to conflate, invert, paraphrase, or otherwise modify them, a kind of freedom common in most of his contemporaries, including Donne himself. Walton is a successful "life writer," not a biographer in the modern sense; for his work is "a precursor of modern biography . . .

more open, ambiguous . . . and potentially more artificial than the modern one" (Anderson, 56).

Walton managed to write his *Lives* in a dramatic mode in which his heroes often take on saintliness; this is a special kind of achievement, for he actually creates believable saints. In his thoughtful study of "Time in Walton's *Lives*," W. Gerald Marshall sees the hagiographer at work: "Walton wishes his audience to admire his subjects not only for their literary, political, or homiletical skills, but also for their ability to render as holy the minutes and the hours, the events and the duties that form the average day. . . . [T]hrough the extensive treatment of time, the biographer now depicts the saint primarily as the person who is able, on a day-to-day basis, to transform the mundane into the sacred, to sense the eternal just behind the minute, day, or observance—and to do so without leading a life that is totally cloistered."[35] Such considerations lead to a discernible "Waltonian" style, the analysis of which has eluded most critics, who are generally rather imprecise in discussing its basis and effect. One notion is that Walton was not quite certain whether he was writing prose to be read silently or something to be spoken aloud. In any event, Walton's style, we have been told, depends on "the old-fashioned kind of prose which can be broken up into parallel and parenthesis, but otherwise seems almost formless to a modern reader. . . . [L]ove of artificial balance as a literary ornament . . . [is] a marked feature of his style. . . . This love of balance even leads him at times perilously close to circumlocution."[36] The judgment seems just, if also general.

James Russell Lowell records somewhat similar impressions about Walton's prose, particularly of the *Lives*. He recalls Walton's comment about his "artless pencil" and his frequent apologies for his literary inadequacy. "But this deprecation," Lowell says, "may have been merely a shiver of his habitual modesty, or, as is more likely, a device of his literary adroitness. . . . Walton, at any rate, in course of time, attained, at least in prose, to something which, if it may not be called style, was a very charming way of writing, all the more so that he has an innocent air of not knowing how it is done. . . . [N]o man ever achieved, as Walton did, a simplicity which leaves criticism helpless, by the mere light of nature alone" (Lowell, 78–79). Although Lowell concedes that Walton was no poet, he does conclude that the poetic element plays an important part in the attractiveness of Walton's prose; for "Walton's prose owes much of its charm to the poetic sentiment in him which was denied a refuge in verse, and . . . his practice in metres may have given to his happier periods a measure and a music they would otherwise have wanted. . . . [H]e loved poetry, and the poetry he loved was generally good. He had also some critical judgment in it" (Lowell, 86). Lowell points out Walton's love for the homely and familiar and his artlessness, which is not quite artless, as sources of the charm of Walton's manner. He is not surprised that Dr. Johnson expressed so much appreciation for the *Lives:* "In reading Walton's *Lives* (and no wonder Johnson loved them so), I have a feeling that I have met him in the street and am hearing them from his own lips" (Lowell, 92). He concludes that Gray also showed his love for them, and that his "Ode on a Distant Prospect of Eton College" was suggested by a passage in the *Life of Wotton* (Lowell, 92n). Lowell is not blind to weaknesses in Walton's style, calling Walton's inconsistency "a genius for rambling" (Lowell, 93). Nevertheless, Lowell approves of Walton because "he praises a meditative life, and with evident sincerity; but we feel that he liked nothing so well as good talk" (Lowell, 110). Finally, as if to corroborate Lowell, in 1899 Austin Dobson also edited the *Angler.* Dobson himself is moved by "the Walton of the cheerful spirit and the clean modesty,—of the frank old words that smell of the soil and the fresh-turned furrows."[37]

Perhaps we might situate Walton scholarship in three stages: the first is largely biographical and genealogical, beginning with William Oldys and Sir John Hawkins, culminating in the work of Sir Nicholas Harris Nicolas; the second is bibliographical, owing much to Hawkins and Nicolas, but more especially to Bethune; the third, textual and stylistic, often illuminates our understanding of Walton's literary skill, his handling of sources, and his political and social context in ways previous writers sometimes miss. Recent work on Walton should not dull one's appreciation of earlier scholarship, however quaint and old fashioned it may now seem. If it was a frequent fault of earlier critics to think Walton less intellectual, less shrewd, and less sophisticated than in fact he was— his reputation for simplicity, modesty, and honesty clings tiresomely— there is currently a tendency to find him a subtle contriver and artificer, one who delights in "artifice for artifice's sake" (Goldman, 188n).

John Buchan reflects the first and much of the second stage of writing about Walton's *Compleat Angler*, which he calls England's perfect pastoral: "The pastoral drama, really a lost art since Theocritus, in spite of Roman, Italian, and Elizabethan revivals, is here restored in all its fresh and courtly grace. It is this which has made the book immortal, for while Maudlin and Coridon sing their catches in the meadow the world will always have ears for their singing." Walton possesses "ease and charm," his style is "crisp," his real purpose to provide "a transcript of old English country life, a study of the folk-heart" (Buchan, xxi). But recent responses to Walton reflect discourse and genre theory and discover in *The Compleat Angler* not so much a fishing manual as a complex and concealed exhibition of literary types and a study of society. According to these views, Walton is making over the kinds of discourse on which community is based. His is a conduct book, an example of meditational literature, and a lyric evocation of social order. We learn, for example, that his literary art is based on subtle modulations from topic to topic, in which he assembles social differences by making use of many different themes, genres, and forms:

> In addressing problems of difference, he adopts generic strategies as various as the materials he combines: accretion (natural histories, lyrics, occasional meditations), modulation (georgic and pastoral), inversion (sacred parody, Lucianic dialogue), alterity (menippean satire). In the interest of contesting contestation, relations among a whole range of genres are transformed. Predicated on mixture and change, Walton's discourse avoids the dilemma of unspeakable foundational questions: values are established through a dialectical play of differences.[38]

We can hardly recognize simple "honest Izaak" from such refined judgments.

To follow the long trail of references to Walton's works, or the numerous ways in which later writers have adapted his *Compleat Angler* or his various *Lives,* would be an impossibly long journey. But I have attempted to show the enduring interest in his life and work, and the variety of interpretations that readers have brought to it. Yet Walton's influence is far reaching indeed, and many of its occasions may await discovery. Perhaps Henry David Thoreau's alleged indebtedness to the *Angler* may be one of these revelations. Can it be that Thoreau's *A Week on the Concord and Merrimack Rivers* shares with Walton's *Angler* "a basic similarity in narrative structure"?[39] More recently, may we see that Graham Greene in *The Power and the Glory* (1940) alludes to Walton through naming Mr. Tench, the dentist who maneuvers the priest's progress? The tench is a common English freshwater fish, but Walton writes of its significance as "the Physician of fishes, for the *Pike* especially, and . . . the *Pike*, being either sick or hurt, is cured by the touch of the *Tench*. And it is observed, that the Tyrant *Pike* will not be a Wolf to his Physician, but forbears to devour him though he be never so hungry." In the novel, Mr. Tench's bondage lies in his relationship with "the tyrant of the waters."[40] Most admirers of Walton, past and present, might agree with the modern judgment that no contradiction exists between his "legendary simplicity and a love of language which made him strive for perfection of style. . . . The important thing to be borne in mind is that a man may be very simple and direct in his outlook on life, very modest, childlike in his attitude toward both spiritual and temporal authority, and yet extremely painstaking and meticulous in cultivation of one of the fine arts" (Goldman, 187n). A natural genius like Izaak Walton is not necessarily naive. In his "study to be quiet," Walton is making a conscious effort to be both contemplative and active, serene and urgent. Indeed, the scriptural phrase that Walton adopts as a kind of motto is a call to holiness, but it is also a warning for all people to be prepared for the last day when the trumpet sounds.

Notes and References

Chapter One

1. Like all recent compilers of Walton's biography, I am indebted to Arthur M. Coon, "The Life of Izaak Walton" (Ph.D. diss., Cornell University, 1938); hereafter cited in the text as Coon.

2. Anthony à Wood, *Athenae Oxoniensis,* 2 vols., 1691–1692, 1:699, observed: "He hath written the lives of Dr. John. Donne, sir Hen. Wotton, Mr. Rich. Hooker, Mr. George Herbert, and of Dr. Rob. Sanderson sometimes B. of Lincoln. All which are well done, considering the education of the author." Wood is hereafter cited in the text.

3. See Izaak Walton, *The Lives of John Donne, Sir Henry Wotton, Richard Hooker, George Herbert and Robert Sanderson,* ed. George Saintsbury (London: Oxford University Press, 1927), 379; hereafter cited in the text as *Lives.* This edition reprints the 1675 edition of the first four *Lives* and the 1678 edition of the last, that is, of Sanderson.

4. See Elias Ashmole, *History of the Order of the Garter* (London, 1672), 228, and cf. Coon, 168, who quotes this passage from Ashmole, and Nicholas Harris Nicolas, *The Lives of Walton and Cotton* (London: William Pickering, 1837), xxxvi–xxxvii, who comments on it.

5. For a reprint of these letters, see Sir Nicholas Harris Nicolas, ed., *The Complete Angler, or The Contemplative Man's Recreation . . . Written by Izaak Walton, and Instructions How to Angle for a Trout or Grayling in a Clear Stream, by Charles Cotton,* 2 vols. (London: Pickering, 1836), 217–18. Coon also reprints the letters in full (299–303).

6. Cotton is writing near the beginning of this second part of the *Angler.* I quote from the Nelson Classics edition (Edinburgh, n.d.), 225.

7. Quoted from *The Compleat Walton,* ed. Geoffrey Keynes (London: Nonesuch Press, 1929), 587–89, ll. 1–6. Line numbers are cited hereafter in the text.

8. One of the best recent descriptions of the Great Tew circle is by Hugh Trevor-Roper, *Catholics, Anglicans and Puritans: Seventeenth-Century Essays* (London: Secker & Warburg, 1987), chap. 4.

9. Walton collected material for a life of John Hales (1584–1656), but it is unlikely that he himself planned to write this life, assuming rather that it was the task of William Fulman of Corpus Christi College, Oxford. See John Butt, "Izaak Walton's Collections for Fulman's Life of John Hales," *Modern Language Review* 29 (1934): 267–73, and Jonquil Bevan, "Izaak Walton's Collections for Fulman's Life of John Hales: The Walker Part," *Bodleian Library*

Record 13 (April 1989): 160–71. I have described the significance of the "ever memorable" John Hales in *Dictionary of Literary Biography: British Prose Writers of the Early Seventeenth Century,* ed. Clayton D. Lein (Detroit: Gale Research, 1995), 151:170–73.

10. See British Library Additional Manuscripts 5088, fols. 139–46.

11. "I only knew Ben Johnson: but my Lord of Winton [that is, George Morley] knew him very well, says he was in the 6°, that is the uppermost fforme in Westminster Schole. At which time his father dyed, and his mother married a brickelayer, who made him (much against his will) to help him in his trade. But in a short time, his scole maister, Mr. Camden, got him a better imployment, which was, to atend or accompany a son of Sir Walter Rauleyes in his travills. Within a short time after their returne, they parted (I think not in cole bloud) and with a love sutable to what they had in their travills (not to be comended) and then Ben began to set up for himself in the trade by which he got his subsistance and fame. Of which I nede not give any account. He got in time to have 100 pounds a year from the King, also a pention from the Cittie, and the like from many of the nobility, and some of the gentry, which was well payd for love or fere of his raling in verse or prose, or boeth. My Lord of Winton told me, he told him he was (in his long retyrement and sickness, when he saw him, which was often) much afflickted that hee had profain'd the scripture in his playes; and lamented it with horror; yet, that at that time of his long retyrement, his pentions (so much as came yn) was given to a woman that govern'd him, with whom he livd and dyed nere the Abie in West minster; and that nether he nor shee tooke much care for next weike, and wood be sure not to want wine; of which he usually tooke too much before he went to bed, if not oftner and soner." See Aubrey's *Brief Lives,* ed. Oliver Lawson Dick (1949; rept. Ann Arbor: University of Michigan Press, 1957), 179–80.

12. H. J. Oliver argues that Walton in fact wrote *Thealma and Clearchus.* See his "Izaak Walton As Author of *Love and Truth* and *Thealma and Clearchus,*" *Review of English Studies* 25 (1949): 24–37. Cf. chap. 3, 57–58, and 17n.

13. A facsimile of Walton's will is published in *The Compleat Angler,* ed. G. A. B. Dewar (London: Freemantle, 1902), between pp. xliv and xlv. It is reprinted in *Waltoniana: Inedited Remains in Verse and Prose of Izaak Walton,* ed. Richard Herne Shepherd (London: Pickering, 1878), item 19.

14. See Hugh A. L. Rice, *Thomas Ken: Bishop and Non-Juror* (London: SPCK, 1958, 1964), 62–63.

15. Walton writes about having discharged a debt of Dorothy Smith's husband, now deceased, some 20 years past, to the Duke of Ormond, who used the money (£150) to purchase "Ensignes and flags and such utensells for war." Walton says that the sum was "paide by the dukes order for his use about the yere. 1641. it was paide (and I thinke by me) to an Agent of my Lords." Walton writes further that

Tho I am a stranger almost to your selfe, yet for your Husbands sake, who was my dere frend, I am willing this my trew testimony may doe you good: and espetially at this time when it seemes you are in necessitie. Now that it may doe that which I intend, and because the duke can have noe knoledg of me to incline him to beleiue me; if his grace will apoynt some one of his atendants to show this my Letter to my Lord the Bishop of Worster, I thinke he will boeth say he knowes this to be my hand, and that he thinkes I am an honest man. I wish your buissnes or any thing that at any time may concerne my selfe may soe prosper, as I conceue I haue spoke the trewth beyond this I shall not inlarge my selfe, Almightie god keepe the duke and you and all that loue him, in his fauor.

The letter is dated at "Worster 21. of March 1661" and signed "Your lo[ving] Frend Izaak: Walton."

On the verso of the letter, Walton adds in a postscript (not shown here) that he thinks he may have "some papers that be not now with me that may give notice to whome 'twas paid: but, doubtles Buffe-Cotes, and ensignes were bought with it, and for my Lord of ormands use. I am not in health and therefore beg to be excused for my bad writing. Iz: Wa."

Chapter Two

1. See Logan Pearsall Smith, *The Life and Letters of Sir Henry Wotton*, 2 vols. (Oxford: Clarendon Press, 1907), 2:358, Wotton to the earl of Cork, from Eton College, 5 December 1635.

2. See Smith, 2:404: "To Iz. Walton, in answer of a letter requesting him to perform his promise of writing the Life of Dr. Dunne."

3. See Donald A. Stauffer, *English Biography Before 1700* (Cambridge, Mass.: Harvard University Press, 1930; rept. New York: Russell and Russell, 1964), who reviews many of the works that Walton would have known. Chapter 4 is devoted entirely to Walton. I am also generally indebted to the more recent work of Richard Wendorf, especially his " 'Visible Rhetorick': Izaak Walton and Iconic Biography," *Modern Philology* 85 (1985): 269–91, much expanded in his book, *The Elements of Life: Biography and Portrait-Painting in Stuart and Georgian England* (Oxford: Clarendon Press, 1990).

4. See Richard Sylvester, "Cavendish's Life of Wolsey: The Artistry of a Tudor Biographer," *Studies in Philology* 57 (1960): 44–71; "Roper's Life of More," in *Essential Articles for the Study of Thomas More,* ed. R. S. Sylvester and G. P. Marc'hadour (Hamden, Conn.: Archon Books, 1977), 189–97; and Wendorf 1985, 270–77. Cavendish's *Wolsey* did not appear in print until 1641, Roper's *More* not until 1626.

5. See David Novarr, *The Making of Walton's "Lives"* (Ithaca, N.Y.: Cornell University Press, 1958), 124–26; hereafter cited in the text as Novarr.

6. Helen Gardner convincingly challenges Walton's account of Donne's death, noting the extreme improbability of a man near death standing balanced on a small urn, with his feet together, hands folded, and eyes closed; "the charcoal fires are a delicious touch, giving *vraisemblance*," but there is no reason to accept literally Walton's zealous description. See "Dean Donne's Monument in St. Paul's," in *Evidence in Literary Scholarship: Essays in Memory of James Marshall Osborn,* ed. René Wellek and Alvaro Riberio (Oxford: Clarendon Press, 1979), 29–44, esp. 35 and 16n; cf. the discussion in chap. 5, pp. 93–94 and 30n.

7. The notes are fully described by Coon, 139–40, and in Novarr, Appendix A, 499–502. These notes are similar to the kind Walton made for a proposed life (not his) of John Hales. See John Butt, "Izaak Walton's Collections for Fulman's Life of John Hales," *Modern Language Review* 29 (1934): 266–73.

8. See *Holy Dying,* ed. P. G. Stanwood (Oxford: Clarendon Press, 1989), 236.

9. *The Compleat Angler, 1653–1676,* ed. Jonquil Bevan (Oxford: Clarendon Press, 1983), 76; the passage remains almost unchanged in the 1676 edition (Bevan, 205–6).

10. Donne closes one of his verse epistles to Sir Henry Wotton, written about the time of his first return to England, with the admiring lines that might embody also Walton's sentiments:

> But, Sir, I'advise not you, I rather doe
> Say o'er those lessons, which I learn'd of you:
> Whom, free from German schismes, and lightnesse
> Of France, and faire Italies faithlesnesse,
> Having from these suck'd all they had of worth,
> And brought home that faith, which you carried forth,
> I throughly love. But if my selfe I'have wonne
> To know my rules, I have, and you have

DONNE.

See *The Satires, Epigrams and Verse Letters,* ed. W. Milgate (Oxford: Clarendon Press, 1967), 73, 225–30nn. I quote ll. 63–71. Cf. Claude Summers and Ted-Larry Pebworth, "Donne's Correspondence with Wotton," *John Donne Journal* 10 (1991): 1–36.

11. See also the modern edition by Milgate, 75–76, cited in note 10.

12. Novarr discusses these parallels at some length in *The Making of Walton's "Lives,"* esp. chap. 5.

Chapter Three

1. See Richard Hooker, *Of the Lawes of Ecclesiastical Politie* (London: Andrew Crooke, 1662), 1 (B1r); hereafter I cite Gauden's "Life and Death of Mr. Richard Hooker" as Gauden, with page and signature, in the text.

2. For a detailed discussion, see my textual introduction to Richard Hooker, *Of the Laws of Ecclesiastical Polity Books VI, VII, VIII,* ed. P. G. Stanwood, The Folger Library Edition of *The Works of Richard Hooker,* vol. 3 (Cambridge, Mass.: Belknap Press of Harvard University Press, 1981), esp. xliv–li.

3. See Hooker, *Laws,* 3:168.

4. In his edition of Richard Hooker's *Works,* John Keble declared that the "Sermon on Pride" and the sermons on Jude were not likely to be Hooker's because they lacked "heightened rhetorical expression" (*The Works of . . . Hooker,* ed. John Keble, 3 vols., 7th ed. (Oxford: Clarendon Press, 1888), 1:liv–lv. Yet the supposedly dubious sermons are in fact by Hooker, who was able to vary his style, depending on the circumstances. See Hooker's *Tractates and Sermons,* ed. Laetitia Yeandle and Egil Grislis, The Folger Library Edition of *The Works of Richard Hooker,* vol. 5 (Cambridge, Mass.: Belknap Press of Harvard University Press, 1990), 299–308.

5. See C. J. Sisson, *The Judicious Marriage of Mr. Hooker* (1940; rept. New York: Octagon Books, 1974).

6. See my study of book 7, cited in note 2, and see also the commentary on this and Hooker's other posthumous books by Arthur Stephen McGrade in the Folger Library Edition of *The Works of Richard Hooker,* vol. 6, part 1 (Binghamton, N.Y.: Medieval and Renaissance Texts and Studies, 1993), 309–83.

7. I am indebted here as elsewhere in this discussion of the *Lives* to Novarr; his chapter "The Life of Herbert" is particularly valuable.

8. See Bevan, ed., *Angler,* 111–12, 259–60.

9. For a descriptive analysis of early Herbert editions, see F. E. Hutchinson, ed., *The Works of George Herbert* (1941; rept. Oxford: Clarendon Press, 1959), lvi–lxv.

10. See Clayton D. Lein, "Art and Structure in Walton's Life of Mr. George Herbert," *University of Toronto Quarterly* 46 (1976): 168.

11. See Amy Charles, *A Life of George Herbert* (Ithaca, N.Y.: Cornell University Press, 1977), 141–45.

12. The phrase is Nicholas Ferrar's, from the account of his life by his brother John. During his last illness, Nicholas is said to have exhorted his family "that they should stedfastly, & constantly adhere to the Doctrine of the Church of England, & to continue in the good old way . . . for it was the true, right, good way to Heaven" (see *The Ferrar Papers,* ed. B. Blackstone [Cambridge: Cambridge University Press, 1938], 38). While John Ferrar's *Life of Nicholas Ferrar* was not printed until 1790, it would be pleasant to suppose that Walton might have seen or known of one of the manuscripts, for the *Life* so well reflects Walton's own disposition and beliefs.

13. Novarr writes convincingly of the political background (see especially, pp. 365–96). See also Robert S. Bosher, *The Making of the Restoration Settlement: The Influence of the Laudians, 1649–1662* (London: Dacre Press, 1951, rev. 1957), esp. chap. 5, "The Exodus of the Presbyterians."

14. On Sanderson's participation in the Savoy Conference and the question of his authorship of the preface to the Book of Common Prayer, see G. J. Cuming, *A History of Anglican Liturgy* (London: Macmillan, 1969), 136–67.

15. See Novarr, 476–80, and esp. his article "Izaak Walton, Bishop Morley, and *Love and Truth*," *Review of English Studies,* n.s. 2 (1951): 30–39.

16. See *Love and Truth* (London: Henry Brome, 1680), 28; hereafter cited in the text.

17. A further work has sometimes been attributed to Walton: *Thealma and Clearchus: A Pastoral History* (London: Benjamin Tooke, 1683); according to the title page, it was written by John Chalkhill, "An Acquaintant and Friend of Edmund Spencer." Walton certainly wrote the preface to this work, dated 7 May 1678, but he cannot be the author of it. See Bevan, ed., *Angler,* 393n. H. J. Oliver, "Izaak Walton as Author of *Love and Truth* and *Thealma and Clearchus,*" cited in chap. 2, note 10, makes an interesting but finally inconclusive case for Walton's authorship. *Thealma and Clearchus* is reprinted in George Saintsbury, *Minor Poets of the Caroline Period,* 3 vols. (1921; rept. Oxford: Clarendon Press, 1968), 2:367–443. Saintsbury gives a valuable description of the provenance of this poem, so far as it can be ascertained. It is most unlikely that Walton would have composed a poem of more than 3,000 lines in his old age—or at any time in his life.

Chapter Four

1. "The scalie herd, more pleasure tooke, / Bath'd in thy dish, then in the brooke" (ll. 27–28), in *Poems* (1640).

2. The lines are quoted from "The Grasse-hopper. To my Noble Friend, Mr. Charles Cotton," in *Lucasta* (1649). See *The Poems of Richard Lovelace,* ed. C. H. Wilkinson (Oxford: Clarendon Press, 1930), 38–40.

3. See *Holy Living,* ed. P. G. Stanwood (Oxford: Clarendon Press, 1989), 5. The extracts from Marvell occur in "Upon Appleton House," stanza 96, and "The Garden," l. 57, in *Poems,* ed. H. M. Margoliouth (Oxford: Clarendon Press, 1971), 86, 53. The phrase from Vaughan appears in "The Night," l. 50, in *Poetry and Selected Prose,* ed. L. C. Martin (London: Oxford University Press, 1963), 358–59.

4. See Bevan, ed., *Angler,* 171. I quote always from the 1676 text, the last edition that bears authorial revision, except where otherwise stated.

5. Jonquil Bevan provides detailed guidance through these and other angling books before Walton, with an accompanying chart that shows their relationship to one another. See Bevan, ed., *Angler,* esp. 15–33.

6. Hesiod, one of the oldest known Greek poets, having lived about 700 B.C., is the author of *Works and Days.* Vergil (70–19 B.C.) describes his georgics as "Hesiodic." See the valuable study of the georgic tradition and Walton's imputed relationship to it by John R. Cooper, *The Art of "The Compleat Angler"* (Durham, NC: Duke University Press, 1968), 30–58; hereafter cited in the text as Cooper.

7. See Henry Reynolds, "Mythomystes" (?1633), in *Critical Essays of the Seventeenth Century,* ed. J. E. Spingarn (London: Oxford University Press, 1908), 1:163; hereafter cited in the text as Reynolds.

8. Yet Walton quotes from the same author's *Purple Island* (1633), canto 12, stanzas 3, 5, and 6, which are in fact in praise of the shepherd's life. See *Poetical Works of Giles and Phineas Fletcher,* ed. F. S. Boas (Cambridge: Cambridge University Press, 1901), vol. 2.

9. See, for example, Conrad Heresbach, *Thereutices,* appended to *Rei rusticae* (1570), [William Samuel,] *Arte of Angling* (1577), and cf. Bevan, ed., *Angler,* intro. and notes.

10. Because Walton himself is content, he is especially able to express contentment. See the appreciative evocation of this ability in "Walton's Wisdom in The Compleat Angler" by G. D'Hangest, *Études Anglaises* 63 (1976): 173–80, which appeared as "La sagesse de Walton dans The Compleat Angler" (an essay in a special issue, *De Shakespeare à T. S. Eliot: Mélanges offers a Henri Fluchère*): "Il importe de dire que la sagesse dont son livre rayonne a sa source dans l'heureux caractère d'un homme, dans sa capacité d'accueillir joyeusement les plaisirs quotidiens de la vie, dans la simplicité de ses goûts, dans sa disposition contemplative aussi" (173–74). ("It is important to say that the wisdom which shines from the work originates in the happy character of the man, in his ability to welcome joyously the daily pleasures of life, in the simplicity of his tastes, and also in his contemplative disposition.")

11. The passage quoted here appears in the first edition of 1653; it is expanded and embellished in later editions, but still it retains essentially the same terms.

12. While he was still bishop of St. David's, the future archbishop of Canterbury participated in a controversy, encouraged by King James, with a well-known Jesuit called Fisher. Laud defined the normative position of the Church of England by claiming the validity of its orders and the apostolic succession of its bishops, and by affirming its belief in the scriptures, the creeds, and the first four general councils of the early and undivided church. The full text of this work first appeared in 1639 (twice) and subsequently in 1673 and 1686 (rept. in Laud's *Works,* in "The Library of Anglo-Catholic Theology" [Oxford: Parker, 1849], vol. 57). Laud's younger contemporary and follower John Cosin, who would become the Restoration bishop of Durham, wrote a number of treatises in which he expresses similar views. For the works noted in the text, see *Works . . . of John Cosin* (Oxford: Parker, 1851), in "The Library of Anglo-Catholic Theology," esp. 4:332–69. Richard Mountague (1577–1641) was a similarly outspoken defender of the Church of England, who aroused enormous opposition in the Puritan Parliament. Charles I, to show his satisfaction with Mountague's views, appointed him in 1628 to the see of Chichester, and in 1638 to Norwich. The quotations are from *Appello Caesarem: A just appeale from two unjust informers* (London, 1625), 134–35.

13.   See the passage from Walton's *Life of Sanderson,* quoted earlier, pp. 81–82, in which Walton displays his anger. Walton's highly partisan views are similar to those of Edward Hyde, earl of Clarendon (1609–1674), whose *History of the Rebellion and Civil Wars in England* (3 vols., 1702–1704) clearly identifies villains (such as Oliver Cromwell) and heroes (such as Charles I).

14.   Nowell did compose two Latin catechisms, but not the one appearing in the Book of Common Prayer, whose author is unknown.

15.   See Anthony Low, "The Compleat Angler's 'Baite'; or, The Subverter Subverted," *John Donne Journal* 4 (1985): 3.

16.   See Low, who writes, "As Walton recognizes, Marlowe and Ralegh inhabit a social world in which debate takes the form of community; but Donne inhabits a private world, in which all argument is reduced to a wonderfully complex yet always self-reflexive 'dialogue of one' " (10).

Chapter Five

1.   See James Russell Lowell, *The Complete Writings of James Russell Lowell* (Cambridge: Riverside Press, 1891), 8:71–112; hereafter cited in the text as Lowell. The quotation appears on p. 75.

2.   See F. G. P. Kellendonk, "Izaak Walton and Sir Henry Wotton's Panegyric of King Charles," *Neophilologus* 61 (1977): 316–20, esp. 316.

3.   See Judith H. Anderson, *Biographical Truth: The Representations of Historical Persons in Tudor-Stuart Writing* (New Haven: Yale University Press, 1984), 55; hereafter cited in the text as Anderson.

4.   See Steven N. Zwicker, *Lines of Authority: Politics and Literary Culture, 1649–1689* (Ithaca, N.Y.: Cornell University Press, 1993), 68; hereafter cited in the text as Zwicker.

5.   See John Butt, "Izaak Walton's Collections for Fulman's Life of John Hales," *Modern Language Review* 29 (1934): 267–73, esp. 269.

6.   See H. J. Oliver, "The Composition and Revisions of 'The Compleat Angler,' " *Modern Language Review* 42 (1947): 295–313, esp. 309.

7.   See B. D. Greenslade, *"The Compleat Angler* and the Sequestered Clergy," *Review of English Studies* 5 (1954): 361–66, esp. 361.

8.   See John Butt, "Izaak Walton's Methods in Biography," *Essays and Studies* 19 (1933): 67–84, esp. 72; hereafter cited in the text as Butt.

9.   See John Buchan, introduction (1901) to *The Compleat Angler,* ed. John Buxton (New York: Oxford University Press, 1982), xvii; hereafter cited in the text as Buchan.

10.   See Nigel Smith, "Oliver Cromwell's Angler," *The Seventeenth Century* 8 (1993): 55–56; hereafter cited in the text as Smith. See also Smith's fascinating study *Literature and Revolution in England, 1640–1660* (New Haven: Yale University Press, 1994), esp. chap. 10, "Calamity As Narrative."

11.   See Novarr, 279–80.

12. See James Boswell, *Life of Johnson,* ed. G. B. Hill (New York: Harper, 1904), 4:360; hereafter cited in the text as Boswell.

13. See Moses Browne, *The Compleat Angler, etc.* (London: H. Kent, 1750), iv–v; hereafter cited in the text as Browne.

14. See Bertram H. Davis, "The Rival Angler Editors: Moses Browne and John Hawkins," in *English Writers of the Eighteenth Century* (New York: Columbia University Press, 1971), 95; hereafter cited in the text as Davis.

15. See Raoul Granqvist, "Izaak Walton's Lives in the Nineteenth and Early Twentieth Century: A Study of a Cult Object," *Studia Neophilologica* 54 (1982): 247–61, esp. 248–49; hereafter cited in the text as Granqvist. Thomas Zouch published his *Life of Walton* in 1826 (London: Thomas Gosden).

16. See William Wordsworth, *The Poetical Works,* ed. Ernest de Selincourt and Helen Darbishire (Oxford: Clarendon Press, 1952–1959), 3:189; hereafter cited in the text as *Poetical Works.*

17. See Wordsworth, *Prose Works,* ed. W. J. B. Owen and J. W. Simpson (Oxford: Clarendon Press, 1974), 2:246–47; hereafter cited in the text as *Prose Works.*

18. See Charles Lamb, *The Letters of Charles and Mary Anne Lamb* (New York: Modern Library, 1935), 214; hereafter cited in the text as Lamb 1935.

19. See Lamb, *Works and Letters,* ed. Edwin W. Marr Jr. (Ithaca, NY: Cornell University Press, 1975), 1:162; hereafter cited in the text as Lamb 1975.

20. See *Letters of William and Dorothy Wordsworth,* ed. Alan G. Hill, 2d ed. (Oxford: Clarendon Press, 1988), 8:110; hereafter cited in the text as *Letters of Wordsworth.*

21. See William Hazlitt, *Complete Works,* ed. P. P. Howe (London: J. M. Dent, 1934), 11:93; hereafter cited in the text as Hazlitt.

22. See *Collected Letters of Samuel Taylor Coleridge,* ed. E. L. Griggs, 4 vols. (Oxford: Clarendon Press, 1956–1959), 1:142.

23. See Abbie Findlay Potts, ed., *The Ecclesiastical Sonnets of William Wordsworth: A Critical Edition* (New Haven: Yale University Press, 1922), 25; hereafter cited in the text as Potts. Wordsworth's sonnet appears on p. 164.

24. See *The Works of . . . Richard Hooker,* ed. John Keble, Rev. R. W. Church, and F. Paget, 7th ed. (Oxford: Clarendon Press, 1888), 1:ix–x.

25. See Sir Nicholas Harris Nicolas, *The Lives of Walton and Cotton* (London: William Pickering, 1837), xxxvii; cited hereafer in the text as Nicolas.

26. See *The Works of the Reverend William Warburton, Lord Bishop of Gloucester* (London, 1788), 7:895.

27. See "The Copy of a Letter writ to Mr. Izaak Walton, by Doctor King," 17 November 1664, which is prefixed to Walton's *Lives,* 15. R. C. Bald reviews Walton's *Life* and its infrequent rivals in *John Donne: A Life* (Oxford: Clarendon Press, 1970), 1–18.

28. See Augustus Jessopp, *John Donne, Sometime Dean of St. Paul's,* Leaders of Religion Series (London, 1897), 217.

29.   See Edmund Gosse, *Life and Letters of John Donne,* 2 vols. (London: Heinemann, 1899), 2:57; hereafter cited in the text as Gosse.

30.   See Helen Gardner, "Dean Donne's Monument in St. Paul's," in *Evidence in Literary Scholarship: Essays in Memory of James Marshall Osborn,* ed. René Wellek and Alvaro Riberio (Oxford: Clarendon Press, 1979), 29–44, esp. 29; hereafter cited in the text.

31.   See Marcus Selden Goldman, "Izaak Walton and The Arte of Angling," in *Studies in Honor of T. W. Baldwin,* ed. Don Cameron Allen (Urbana: University of Illinois Press, 1958), 185–86, 230; hereafter cited in the text as Goldman.

32.   See Bernard S. Horne, *The Compleat Angler, 1653–1967: A New Bibliography* (Pittsburgh: University of Pittsburgh Press, 1970), which is a very full list of translations and editions. But Rodolphe L. Coigney's splendid *Izaak Walton: A New Bibliography, 1653–1987* (New York: James Cummins, 1989) is more complete. Coigney records 456 editions (including translations), from the first of 1653 down to 1988.

33.   See Peter Oliver, *A New Chronicle of The Compleat Angler* (New York: Paisley; London: Williams and Norgate, 1936), x–xi.

34.   See especially Jonquil Bevan's careful study of Walton's sources in her edition of *The Compleat Angler,* 15–33.

35.   See W. Gerald Marshall, "Time in Walton's Lives," *Studies in English Literature* 32 (1992): 429–42; the quotations appear on pp. 429–30 and 439–40.

36.   See H. J. Oliver, "Izaak Walton's Prose Style," *Review of English Studies* 21 (1945): 280–88, esp. 284–85.

37.   See Austin Dobson, "On Certain Quotations in Walton's 'Angler,' " in Dobson, *Miscellanies* (1901; rept. New York: Dodd, Mead, 1967), 2:169.

38.   See David Hill Radcliffe, " 'Study to be Quiet': Genre and Politics in Izaak Walton's Compleat Angler," *English Literary Renaissance* 22 (1992): 95–111, esp. 110.

39.   See Cliff Toliver, "The Re-creation of Contemplation: Walton's Angler in Thoreau's Week," *ESQ: A Journal of the American Renaissance* 38 (1992): 292–313, esp. 305.

40.   See D. P. Thomas, "Mr. Tench and Secondary Allegory in *The Power and the Glory,*" *English Language Notes* 7 (1969): 129–33. *The Compleat Angler* is quoted from Jonquil Bevan's edition, 308.

Selected Bibliography

PRIMARY SOURCES

The Compleat Angler

The Compleat Angler, or the Contemplative Man's Recreation. Being a Discourse of Fish and Fishing, Not unworthy the perusal of most Anglers. London: Richard Marriot, 1653. Revised as *The Compleat Angler, or the Contemplative Man's Recreation. Being a Discourse of Rivers, and Fish-Ponds, and Fish, and Fishing. Not unworthy of the perusal of most Anglers*. London: Richard Marriot, 1655. Further revised as *The Compleat Angler, or the Contemplative Man's Recreation. Being a Discourse of Rivers, Fish-Ponds, Fish and Fishing. To which Is added The Laws of Angling: with a new Table of the Particulars in this Book*. London: Richard Marriot, 1661, 1668. Finally revised as *The Universal Angler, Made so, by Three Books of Fishing. The First Written by Mr. Izaak Walton; The Second by Charles Cotton, Esq.; The Third by Col. Robert Venables*. London: Richard Marriot, 1676.

The Compleat Angler, 1653–1676. Ed. Jonquil Bevan. Oxford: Clarendon Press, 1983. The best modern edition, collated and annotated, with detailed description of the five editions (as in the previous entry).

The Lives

Since Walton was continuously revising his *Lives,* their bibliography is very complicated. Novarr (see Secondary Sources) clarifies the dating and the relationship of the various revisions of the five *Lives.*

Donne, John. *Poems. With elegies on the author's death*. London: John Marriot, 1633. Twelve elegies appear in this edition, including Walton's. All the elegies but one, with an additional three, appeared in the second edition of 1635; they are reprinted in Grierson, cited later.

———. *The Poems of John Donne*. Ed. H. J. C. Grierson. 2 vols. London: Oxford University Press, 1912, 1:379–95. Reprints Walton's "Elegie upon Dr. Donne."

The Life of John Donne, Dr. in Divinity, and Late Dean of Saint Pauls Church London. London: Richard Marriot, 1658. Revised edition of "The Life and Death of Dr Donne, Late Deane of St Pauls London," which appeared in

LXXX Sermons preached by that learned and reverend divine, Iohn Donne, Dr in Divinity, Late Deane of the Cathedrall Church of S. Pauls London. London: Richard Royston and Richard Marriot, 1640.

The Life of Sir Henry Wotton. London: Richard Marriot, 1651. This appeared in *Reliquiae Wottonianae,* edited by Walton (1651, 1654, 1672 with a revised "Life").

The Life of Mr. Rich. Hooker, The Author of those Learned Books of the Laws of Ecclesiastical Polity. London: Richard Marriot, 1665. Revised in *The Works of Mr. Richard Hooker.* London: Andrew Crooke, 1666.

The Life of Mr. George Herbert. London: Richard Marriot, 1670, 1674 (included in Herbert's *Temple*).

The Lives of Dr. John Donne, Sir Henry Wotton, Mr. Richard Hooker, Mr. George Herbert. London: Richard Marriot, 1670, 1675. The collected *Lives,* excluding that of Sanderson, which is first added in the edition by Thomas Zouch (1796).

The Life of Dr. Sanderson, Late Bishop of Lincoln. To which is added, some short Tracts or Cases of Conscience, written by the said Bishop. London: Richard Marriot, 1678. Revised in *XXXV Sermons,* by Robert Sanderson. 7th ed. London: Benjamin Tooke, 1681.

The Lives of John Donne, Sir Henry Wotton, Richard Hooker, George Herbert and Robert Sanderson. The World's Classics 303. Ed. George Saintsbury. London: Oxford University Press, 1927. Reprints *The Lives of Dr. John Donne, Sir Henry Wotton, Mr. Richard Hooker, Mr. George Herbert* (1670) and *The Life of Dr. Sanderson* (1678). This edition, the most convenient modern one, has been frequently reprinted.

The Compleat Walton. Ed. Geoffrey Keynes. London: Nonesuch Press, 1929.

Other Works

"An Elegie upon Dr. Donne." In *Poems, By J.D. with Elegies on the Authors Death.* London: John Marriot, 1633. Rev. 1635.

"To my ingenious Friend Mr. Brome, on his various and excellent Poems: An humble Eglog. Daman and Dorus. Written the 29. of May, 1660." In *Songs and Other Poems,* by Alexander Brome. London: Henry Brome, 1661.

Love and Truth: in two modest and peaceable letters. London: Henry Brome, 1680.

Thealma and Clearchus, a Pastoral History. Preface by Walton. London: Benjamin Tooke, 1683.

Waltoniana: Inedited Remains in Verse and Prose of Izaak Walton. Ed. Richard Herne Shepherd. London: Pickering, 1878.

SECONDARY SOURCES

Bibliography

Butt, John. "Lives." *Proceedings of the Oxford Bibliographical Society* 2.4 (1930): 327–40. Describes the seventeenth-century editions of the *Lives.*

Coigney, Rodolphe L. *Izaak Walton: A New Bibliography, 1653–1987.* New York: Cummins, 1989. The most recent bibliography, supplementing Horne, cited later.

Donovan, Dennis G. "Izaak Walton." *English Literary Renaissance* 1 (1971): 300–303. An annotated bibliography of studies to 1970, which is continued by Andrea Sununu, cited later.

Horne, Bernard S. *The Compleat Angler, 1653–1967: A New Bibliography.* Pittsburgh: University of Pittsburgh Press, 1970. Includes a descriptive list of publishers' bindings.

Oliver, Peter. *A New Chronicle of "The Compleat Angler."* New York: Paisley, 1936. Examines the reprinting history of *The Compleat Angler.*

Sununu, Andrea. "Izaak Walton (1970–1985)." *English Literary Renaissance* 17 (1987): 251–55. Continues Donovan, cited previously.

Biography and Criticism

Bevan, Jonquil. "Izaak Walton and His Publisher." *The Library* 5th ser., 32 (1977): 344–59. An examination of Walton's relationship with his long-time friend and publisher, Richard Marriot.

———. *Izaak Walton's "The Compleat Angler": The Art of Recreation.* Brighton, Sussex: Harvester, 1988. A brief but instructive introduction to Walton's life, times, and principal work, with useful bibliography.

———. "Henry Valentine, John Donne and Izaak Walton." *Review of English Studies,* n.s. 40 (1989): 179–201. Fascinating study of Valentine, Donne's assistant at St. Dunstan's, later vicar of St. Nicholas's, Deptford, and Walton's nephew-in-law.

———. "Izaak Walton's Collections for Fulman's Life of John Hales: The Walker Part." *Bodleian Library Record* 13 (April 1989): 160–71. An addition to the documents transcribed by John Butt (1934), cited in the following entry.

Butt, John. "Izaak Walton's Collections for Fulman's Life of John Hales." *Modern Language Review* 29 (1934): 266–73. A discussion and a transcription of Walton's notes for the unwritten biography of John Hales.

———. *Biography in the Hands of Walton, Johnson, and Boswell.* Ewing Lectures. Los Angeles: University of California, 1966. Discusses Walton's use of anecdote and comments on his biographical style in the *Lives.*

————. *Pope, Dickens and Others: Essays and Addresses.* Edinburgh: Edinburgh University Press, 1969. Reprints the Ewing Lecture on Walton as "Izaak Walton As Biographer."

Coon, Arthur M. "The Life of Izaak Walton." Ph.D. diss., Cornell University, 1938. Still the fullest and best biographical study of Walton, his family, and his connections.

Cooper, John R. *The Art of "The Compleat Angler."* Durham, NC: Duke University Press, 1968. An important study of Walton's traditions, especially the georgic and pastoral modes, and his borrowings of classical and contemporary literature.

Costa, Francisque. *L'Oeuvre d'Izaak Walton (1593–1683).* Études Anglaises 48. Paris: Didier, 1973. Substantial, often speculative study of the life, works, and social and ecclesiastical background. Includes a useful bibliography, especially of works related to the seventeenth-century background.

D'Hangest, G. "La sagesse de Walton dans *The Compleat Angler.*" *Études Anglaises* 63 (1976): 173–80. A special issue, *De Shakespeare à T. S. Eliot: Mélanges offerts a Henri Fluchère.* An evocative portrayal of Walton's central desire, to "study to be quiet."

Epstein, William H. *Recognizing Biography.* Philadelphia: University of Pennsylvania Press, 1987. On the nature and theory of biographical writing; chapter 2, "Altering the Life-Text," deals with the *Life of Donne.*

Fehner, Richard E. "Izaak Walton's *Life of Sir Henry Wotton,* 1651, 1654, 1670, 1672, 1675: A Study of Sources, Revisions, and Chronology." Ph.D. diss., University of Minnesota, 1961. An important and detailed study and comparison of the different versions of the *Life of Wotton,* corroborating and supplementing Novarr (cited later). Contains bibliography.

Gardner, Helen. "Dean Donne's Monument in St. Paul's." In *Evidence in Literary Scholarship: Essays in Memory of James Marshall Osborn.* Ed. René Wellek and Alvaro Riberio. Oxford: Clarendon Press, 1979, 29–44. Challenges the credibility of Walton's story of Donne's posing in his shroud.

Gauden, John. "The Life and Death of Mr. Richard Hooker." In *The Works of Mr. Richard Hooker.* London: Andrew Crook, 1662. The biography that encouraged Walton's "revised" *Life.*

Granqvist, Raoul. "Izaak Walton's *Lives* in the Nineteenth and the Early Twentieth Century: A Study of a Cult Object." *Studia Neophilogica* 54 (1982): 247–61. An important study of the publishing history of Walton's *Lives.*

Haskin, Dayton. "A History of Donne's 'Canonization' from Izaak Walton to Cleanth Brooks." *Journal of English and Germanic Philology* 92 (1993): 17–36. Describes the "new criticism" in light of Walton's biography of Donne.

Lambert, Lionel. *Izaak Walton and the Royal Deanery of Stafford.* Stafford: J. & C. Mort, 1926. A detailed, antiquarian description of the city of Walton's birth and early years, with illustrations.

Lein, Clayton D. "Art and Structure in Walton's *Life of Mr. George Herbert.*" *University of Toronto Quarterly* 46 (1976): 162–76. Describes the formal structural patterns of the *Life of Herbert*.

———. "Izaak Walton." In *Dictionary of Literary Biography: British Prose Writers of the Early Seventeenth Century.* Vol. 151. Detroit: Gale Research, 1995, 306–21. Useful survey of Walton's life and work, with excellent bibliography.

Low, Anthony. "The Compleat Angler's 'Baite'; or, The Subverter Subverted." *John Donne Journal* 4 (1985): 1–12. Demonstrates the relationship of Donne's "The Baite" to the pastoral strain in *The Compleat Angler.*

Marshall, W. Gerald. "Time in Walton's *Lives.*" *Studies in English Literature* 32 (1992): 429–42. Argues that *time* and *ritual* are the central organizing ideas of the *Lives.*

Martin, Stapleton. *Izaak Walton and His Friends.* London: Chapman & Hall, 1903. An agreeably old-fashioned survey of the life and works, with brief sketches of 26 of Walton's most famous friends; numerous illustrations of persons and places.

Nardo, Anna K. "A recreation of a recreation": Reading *The Compleat Angler.*" *South Atlantic Quarterly* 79 (1980): 302–11. Emphasizes Walton's sense of play and playfulness in his fishing manual.

Novarr, David. "Izaak Walton, Bishop Morley, and *Love and Truth.*" *Review of English Studies,* n.s. 2 (1951): 30–39. Argues convincingly for Walton as author, who is reflecting the principles of the Great Tew circle.

———. *The Making of Walton's "Lives."* Ithaca, N.Y.: Cornell University Press, 1958. The most thorough study of all of Walton's *Lives;* shows how Walton came to compose the biographies and compares the various versions of each one.

Oliver, H.J. "Izaak Walton As Author of *Love and Truth* and *Thealma and Clearchus.*" *Review of English Studies* 25 (1949): 24–37. Claims that Walton is the author certainly of the former and possibly of the latter.

Pamp, Frederic E. "Walton's Redaction of Hooker." *Church History* 17 (1948): 95–116. Conveniently summarizes the circumstances behind Walton's study of Hooker.

Radcliffe, David Hill. " 'Study to be Quiet': Genre and Politics in Izaak Walton's *Compleat Angler.*" *English Literary Renaissance* 22 (1992): 95–111. Develops the implications of Walton's work as a conduct book, as meditational literature, and as a lyric evocation of social order.

Ray, Robert H. "Herbert's Words in Donne's Mouth: Walton's Account of Donne's Death," *Modern Philology* 85 (1987): 186–87. Suggests that Walton ascribes to Donne words that originate in Herbert.

Rewa, Michael P. *Reborn As Meaning: Panegyrical Biography from Isocrates to Walton.* Washington, D.C.: University Press of America, 1963. Sets Walton in the history of life-writing from antiquity through the Christian centuries, concentrating especially (in chapter 5) on the *Life of Donne.*

Smith, Nigel. "Oliver Cromwell's Angler." *Seventeenth Century* 8 (1993): 51–65. On the reception of *The Compleat Angler* in the late Restoration, especially by Richard Franck, who is somewhat dismissive of Walton in his *Northern Memoirs* (1694).

Snader, Joe. "*The Compleat Angler* and the Problems of Scientific Methodology." *John Donne Journal* 12 (1993): 169–89. Argues that Walton's conservative political and religious outlook extends also to his view of the development of scientific methodology, for Walton relies on oral instruction filled with pleasant interludes.

Stauffer, Donald A. *English Biography Before 1700.* Cambridge, Mass.: Harvard University Press, 1930. Rept. New York: Russell and Russell, 1964. A standard survey of biographical methods and writers from the Middle Ages to the end of the seventeenth century; chapter 4 is devoted to Walton.

Toliver, Cliff. "The Re-creation of Contemplation: Walton's *Angler* in Thoreau's *Week.*" *ESQ: A Journal of the American Renaissance* 38 (1992): 292–313. Argues convincingly that Walton influenced the style and structure of Henry David Thoreau's *A Week on the Concord and Merrimack Rivers,* which in turn illuminates *The Compleat Angler.*

Wendorf, Richard. " 'Visible Rhetorick': Izaak Walton and Iconic Biography." *Modern Philology* 85 (1985): 269–91. On verbal portraiture and its relationship to time, point of view, and the presentation of fully developed character.

———. *The Elements of Life: Biography and Portrait-Painting in Stuart and Georgian England.* Oxford: Clarendon Press, 1990. Includes " 'Visible Rhetorick' " but adds a further chapter on Walton; develops the theme of historical character and "iconic portraiture."

Index

The Author

Paul G. Stanwood is professor of English and former director of graduate studies in English at the University of British Columbia. He received his Ph.D. from the University of Michigan–Ann Arbor. He has edited John Cosin's *Collection of Private Devotions;* Henry More's *Democritus Platonissans;* William Law's *Serious Call to a Devout and Holy Life* and *The Spirit of Love* (with Austin Warren); *John Donne and the Theology of Language* (with Heather Ross Asals); Richard Hooker's *Of the Laws of Ecclesiastical Polity* (books 6, 7, and 8); Jeremy Taylor's *Holy Living* and *Holy Dying* (2 vols.); and *Of Poetry and Politics: New Essays on Milton and His World.* He is a contributing editor to the *John Donne Variorum,* in progress, and has written essays on Spenser, Donne, Hooker, Herbert, Taylor, Joseph Beaumont, Cosin, Crashaw, Milton, Christina Rossetti, and T. S. Eliot. He has also published a collection of his essays, entitled *The Sempiternal Season: Studies in Seventeenth-Century Devotional Writing,* and has edited the forthcoming *Selected Prose of Christina Rossetti* (with David A. Kent). He is past president of the John Donne Society of America and currently a member of the executive committee of the International Association of University Professors of English.

The Editor

Arthur F. Kinney is the Thomas W. Copeland Professor of Literary History at the University of Massachusetts, Amherst, and the Director of the Center for Renaissance Studies there; he is also an adjunct professor of English at New York University. He has written several books in the field, including *Humanist Poetics, Continental Humanist Poetics, John Skelton: Priest as Poet* and the forthcoming *Lies Like the Truth: "Macbeth" and the Cultural Moment*. He is the founding editor of the journal *English Literary Renaissance* and editor of the book series "Massachusetts Studies in Early Modern Culture."